I Just Had to Laugh

Amusing Anecdotes, Humorous Stories and
Outrageous Episodes
from 50 years of Priestly Ministry

Rev. J. Ronald Knott

Sophronismos Press
Louisville, Kentucky

I Just Had to Laugh

Amusing Anecdotes, Humorous Stories and Outrageous Episodes from 50 years of Priestly Ministry

Cover Design & Book Layout: Tim Schoenbachler

First Printing: December 2018

ISBN: 978-0-9962445-7-2

Table of Contents

"God has given me reasons to laugh and anyone who hears about this will laugh with me."

Genesis 21:6

Dedication

To

Tom and Rea Clark,

two of the finest people I know.

PREFACE

There is a thin line that separates laughter and pain,
comedy and tragedy, humor and hurt.

Erma Bombeck

No matter where I have been assigned as a priest, I have seen my share of pain, loss and sadness. It goes with being "with people" especially when they experience illnesses, tragedies and deaths. During those moments, I have had the privilege of crying and grieving with them. A few of them are included in this book.

However, that is just one side of the coin. There have very often been moments when I have had the privilege of laughing with them – sometimes in front of them and even sometimes after the fact.

The stories I share in this book are only a few of the many memorable episodes, mostly humorous and sometimes almost unbelievable, that came to mind when I set out to write this book.

I can say, in conclusion, that my fifty years of ministry have been a real blessing. I have probably laughed more than I have cried. Sometimes I laughed at my own self and the predicaments in which I found myself. Sometimes I laughed at the comical things people said to me. At other times, I laughed at the odd and unexpected responses I have gotten from others in situations in which we both found ourselves.

I thank all the people mentioned in this book who have helped me enjoy life so much, especially those who have often had to put up with my quirky personality.

OFF TO A SHAKY START

I was born at home in the town of Rhodelia, Kentucky (population less than 50 including the "suburbs") the early afternoon of April 28, 1944. I was delivered by my grandmother, Lilly Mills Knott, who was a country midwife and who lived across the road from our house. In danger of death, my grandmother baptized me right there on the spot. She, no doubt knew how to do it, because circumstances had required her to do so several times before.

My mother needed glucose, something new in medicine at that time. When the doctor arrived, he realized that he had brought the wrong needle to introduce the IV for the glucose drip. His Model-T Ford car had to make a quick 30 mile round trip back to Brandenburg to retrieve a workable needle.

The amazing thing is that no one bothered to mention my bedside baptism. I only discovered that fact when I asked for a baptismal certificate when I was applying to go to the seminary. My pastor said casually, "Oh, I see your grandmother baptized you "in danger of death" and you were brought to church a few days later for the "ceremonies of the church." I have always been proud of the fact that I was given the "new life of baptism" by the same woman who helped save my life in the process of human birth! I was so proud to see her in the front pews at my First Mass. I always wonder what she was thinking that day as she watched me at the altar.

ENOUGH, ALREADY!

One night after celebrating five Masses on Sunday and delivering five homilies, as I used to do for years when I was Vocation Director and Bellarmine University Campus Minister, I had a very vivid dream. I was standing in silence before God in my vestments. God said to me in a very clear, but weary, voice, “Ron, shut up!”

DOG GONE IT!

One day, a friend and I were sitting on his front porch. He lived on a busy street next to a cemetery wall. We were discussing where we might go for a bite to eat. As we sat there, a small dog came running down the hill on the opposite side of the street. It acted like it was going to try to cross the busy road, so we began yelling and waving our arms trying to keep it from running out into the street. It was a young pup, so instead of running away from us it ran toward us. When we saw it entering the street, we tried to wave at the cars in an attempt to get their attention and to keep them from hitting the dog who was frozen in fear in the middle of the street. It didn’t work. To our horror, one of the cars hit the poor dog. To keep it from being run over again and again, we waited for a break in the traffic and quickly dragged the dead puppy to the sidewalk. We put it in a black garbage bag and let it lay on the grass between the sidewalk and the house. We sat on the porch looking at the bag thinking about what to do next.

Within a minute or two, a young girl came down the hill chanting, “Here Fluffy! Here Fluffy!” We looked at each other with that knowing look that this was not going to turn out well. When she got to the bottom of the hill, she noticed us sitting on the porch. “Have you seen a small white puppy around here?” We looked at each other and pointed to the bag! She stood over the bag and wailed for a few minutes before picking it up and heading back up the hill. As she left, my friend looked over at me and said, "Well, it could have been worse. At least she had a priest and a cemetery right here!"

I learned then that this was not the first neighborhood pet to die in that street. The last time it had been a cat. My friend picked up the dead cat, put it in a garbage bag and threw it in a dumpster. A few days after the tragic incident, the owner came knocking at his door. "Have you seen a tabby cat on the loose recently?" He did not have the heart to tell her what he had done with the cat, so he made up a story. "Yes, your cat was hit by a car. I had just bought a shrub to plant in my back yard, so I dug a hole and put the cat under the shrub. He's buried out back." Since it had been a week, and the weather was hot, she did not request a dis-internment. Instead, for several months afterwards, she would show up at his door with flowers asking if she could place them at the mysterious shrub in the cat's memory.

THE UNKNOWN SOLDIER

I had never conducted a funeral at a military cemetery until the day I was called to say a prayer for an old soldier who was going to be buried in one of our country's military cemeteries. He had lived out of state for many years and had died at a very old age without any relatives young enough and well enough to come to his Kentucky burial.

When I arrived, it had been raining. There were no pall bearers, just myself, the undertaker and a couple of cemetery workers. I helped carry the coffin over to the grave. There was no tent, no chairs, no fake green carpet and no lowering contraption that you normally see – just a hole in the ground. They put the casket on the ground until I finished blessing the grave and commending him to the Lord. Then we were instructed to pick up the casket, stand over the hole and when announced, drop it into the hole.

As it turned out, the grave had been hastily dug, but not long enough for the casket. When we heard "drop it," we all let go. The casket did not go the bottom of the grave. It stuck half-way down, with the head much lower than the feet. We were then instructed to "pull it out and let us shave the side of the grave a bit." We tugged and tugged until we pulled it out while scrapping the paint off the sides of the casket on the way back up. The diggers jumped into the hole and shaved the sides a bit, but not enough. We picked up the scrapped casket, held it over the hole and dropped it again on cue! This time the head went all the way to the bottom, while the feet were up in the air about two feet. We tugged and tugged, trying to extricate the casket from the hole one more time, but to no avail. It was decided to leave the casket up with his feet above his head about two feet. They filled the grave with dirt as I stood there shocked at what had just happened, thanking God there were no living relatives or friends to see what had taken place. To this day, I wonder whether I should have reported it to the Veterans Administration.

WESTWARD, HO!

In the summer of 1968, when I was two years away from ordination to priesthood, I had the opportunity to conquer some of my chronic bashfulness and learn how to preach. The opportunity came from the United Church of Christ of all places. They offered a summer program for student ministers (seminarians) called A Christian Ministry in the National Parks. They would train you, assign you to one of the national parks, and help you find a paying summer job in the park.

I went to Chicago to be trained and was assigned to Crater Lake National Park in Oregon. I was to preach twice a weekend in the campgrounds and I was given the job of night desk clerk at the Lodge.

To get out there, I found a place in Chicago where I could deliver a used Lincoln convertible to Seattle. From there I took a bus down to Crater Lake. I put the top down on the convertible and headed for Washington state. I got a ticket for speeding in Nebraska. I was on the open road with no one in sight – no towns, no cars and no gas stations for miles and miles so I was surprised when a police car showed up in my rear view mirror. Curious about how I was caught, the policeman told me that I was tracked by a helicopter.

When I left Chicago, I forgot to ask how to put the top up on the convertible. I could never figure it out no matter how many times I searched to dashboard. Thank God it never rained. I drove through snow in the mountains of Washington with the top down and ended up with one of the worst colds I have ever had. It was only when I delivered the car that I found out that the button to lower the top of the convertible was inside the glove compartment.

When I got to Crater Lake, around the first of June, snow was all the way up to the second floor of the Lodge. One of my first jobs was to shovel down to the front door. Until the Lodge was open for guests several weeks later, I drove a garbage truck through the campgrounds. I was given a young woman, another student worker, as an assistant. She could not drive the truck or lift the garbage bags and throw them high enough to get them in the truck. I would put the truck in gear, let her steer, while I ran back and threw the garbage bags on the truck and then run and catch up with the truck and jump in to drive it to the next stop until the truck was full. Then we would drive to the dump in the woods to unload it. No sooner than we started unloading the bags, bears would come out of the woods and surrounded the truck. We had to wait until they finished eating what was in the bags before we got down to get back into the truck.

Another job I was given before my main job started was to drive the Lodge limousine to the airport to pick up guests. It was a half hour trip each way.

The limousine was so long that the driver had a microphone he could use to talk to people in the back. I got in the habit of making up “facts” about the park as we drove up to the Lodge. "That rock is the very rock Zebulon Pike stopped at to rest on his way to Pike's Peak!" They would believe anything.

That summer, I was the Master of Ceremonies at the Miss Crater Lake Beauty Pageant. Each entry represented one of the girls from each of the park departments. "Miss Garbage Truck" won that year.

To get home at the end of the summer, I was intending to drive the cab of a fourteen-wheeler back to the Midwest for a trucking company. Instead, one of the students offered me a free car – a 1953 Buick that he had driven from Connecticut to the west coast. He was going to go back on a motorcycle.

The most obvious problem with the car was that a wheel, front right, had come off on the expressway in California and had to be welded back on with no possibility of ever changing that tire. The second problem was that I had to get a push to get it started on a four-day 2,400 mile trip back home.

I decided to try it. I would never stop and turn off the key unless I was on a hill where I could get a push. I had a flat tire in the middle of the prairie in Wyoming somewhere. Luckily enough it was the left front tire. When I got to the top of the bumper jack, I noticed that the car was still on the pavement. The jack had gone down through the plate and into the ground rather than lift the car up. As luck would have it, there was a second jack in the trunk, believe it or not. I could not get the other jack out of the ground and had to go off and leave it in the shoulder, hoping no one would run into it.

Somewhere in Iowa, I inadvertently turned off the key at a restaurant. Coming out after lunch, I could not get the car started. It was a very flat area so I called AAA, even though I was not a member and did not want to pay the fee. Just as the AAA truck pulled into the parking lot, I tried it again and miraculously, it started. I peeled out of that parking lot before the AAA man could come to a stop.

When I got home, I left the car at my parent's house and went back to the seminary just in time to start school. A couple of weeks later, I went home to deal with the car. It never ever started again and had to be hauled to the junkyard.

A month or two later, at the seminary, I got a call that someone downstairs wanted to see me. It was the guy who gave me the car. He was on his motorcycle. He stopped in to see me because he could not believe I made it back to Indiana in that old 1953 Buick! He told me that several of the students had made bets that I would not make it out of Oregon.

I learned that summer that "impossible" things, with a bit of luck and lot of naivete, are possible.

SEMINARY SHENANIGANS

When I first arrived at Saint Meinrad Seminary in 1964 for my third year of college, we were forced to live four to a room with two bunkbeds, four small desks and four chests of drawers. To relieve the stress of being so cramped, we were always pulling tricks on people. One series of tricks involved a life-size statue of Saint Thomas Aquinas.

One evening, I opened the door to my room to see Saint Thomas in my bed with the sheets pulled up to his neck. It really startled me for a few seconds because it looked like a huge swollen corpse.

Another time, there was a knock at my door and when I opened it, there was Saint Thomas standing there with his nose practically on the door. I, of course, nearly jumped out of my skin.

It was not uncommon for a knock on your door and when you opened it, Saint Thomas would roll past you on a set of garbage can rollers.

Before we were allowed to leave campus in our own cars, we were basically locked in. If you did not have a stash of food from home, you were out of luck if you wanted an evening snack. The kitchen was locked after dinner. One night a bunch of us were hungry, so we stole some monk's habits out of the laundry and put them on and walked through the monastery, which was still in the main building, and down to the kitchen. It was dark in the hallways and we put the hoods up, which made us unrecognizable to any monk we would run into. The only thing we could find to "steal" was some government cheese and some homemade bread. When you're that hungry, it tastes like a feast. Getting away with it, made it taste even better.

As the years went by, we got even more nervy and took even greater risks. I remember coming in late one night from a ministry assignment in one of the local parishes. We were hungry. We went into the guest house kitchen which was unlocked. We did not turn on the lights to avoid being discovered. We found some eggs and some bread and decided to cook some egg sandwiches. We turned on the grill, not realizing that it had an aluminum cover on it. We smeared the lid with oil and cracked the eggs onto it. In a few minutes the grill cover started buckling. The eggs all ran to the center and onto the floor. About that time, we heard someone coming so we turned off the grill and ran for our lives. I still wonder what the morning cooks thought when they came into the kitchen the next morning to see a warped gill cover and eggs all over the floor. Thank God there wasn't a "papal investigation and prosecution." No one ever mentioned it.

Probably the most risky thing we ever did was to go to Mardi Gras in New Orleans during retreat week!

I remember someone asking what we could do that weekend. After inquiring about what was available, someone mentioned Mardi Gras. Before you knew it, four of us were borrowing money up and down the hallway for enough money to make the trip.

Even riskier, we went to Notre Dame Seminary in New Orleans, and asked if we could stay a few days. They gave us some guest rooms, but kept looking at us curiously – like "what are you doing here?" Thank God they did not call Saint Meinrad to inquire.

One of the four of us was a monk from Marion Abbey outside Chicago. He was almost kicked out. The rest of us "got away with it" without any repercussions. To this day, I can't believe we did it or got away with it!"

In our first year of theology, we started receiving some of the minor orders which Vatican II eventually did away with: tonsure, acolyte, porter, lector, exorcist and subdeacon.

Tonsure was basically a ceremonial haircut by the archbishop of Indianapolis. The ritual entailed cutting four small snippets of hair on all sides of ones head. In those days, long hair and beards became popular. It was the 1960s. The archbishop of Indianapolis hated long hair. When someone approached him with long hair, instead of cutting snippets, he would cut big gouges. This would insure they would have to get a haircut the next day.

Yes, I am an ordained Exorcist. We were ordained for that purpose, but we were warned never to try to use it. As one of the oldest staff members at Saint Meinrad before I retired, I was the only official Exorcist on the staff. I loved to throw that around with the younger guys.

When it came time to be ordained a deacon, the archbishop was too fragile to come to Saint Meinrad, so we all went to Indianapolis. While we were all lying prostrate on the floor during the Litany of the Saints, a tornado hit Indianapolis. I could hear it. It sounded like a train coming down the street. I always wondered if it was a sign from God that we should be held up for all the stunts we pulled in the seminary.

WHO NOSE?

When I was a transitional deacon, I was sent to a funeral home to say a prayer for a single woman who had never married, who had died in her old age leaving no relatives or friends. There was no funeral Mass. She did not belong to a parish. Someone thought she was a Catholic and that it would be a good idea if a priest would come and say a prayer. I gladly went.

After my prayer, the funeral director, preparing the casket to be sent for burial, started to fold the lining of the casket over the face of the poor old woman while I stood there talking to him. He was looking at me and not paying attention to what he was doing. He lowered the lid, but it did not close so he pushed on it and pushed on it. It still didn't close. Finally, he realized that he had not lowered her head as is customary, so that they look like they are lying on a pillow. When he opened the lid, I noticed that her nose was flattened on her face from his pressure of his pushing down on the lid. He lowered the head rest and closed her casket, flattened nose and all! Thankfully, she had no relatives there to see this.

SAY WHAT?

I was asked to preside at a wedding in the small, isolated rural parish of Clementsville, Kentucky. It was mid-summer and they did not have air-conditioning. Instead they had four huge fans set on the highest speed possible.

I had left the lectionary on the lectern open to the gospel that they had selected. However, the fans had blown the pages over and the readings for a funeral were opened for me instead. I did not notice until I started reading something about "your suffering will soon be over, you will leave this world and you will be freed of your sins." Instead of stopping, I just kept reading until I finished.

I looked up and noticed that no one realized it but me. As I suspected, no one was paying attention so I saw no need to admit my mistake.

SHE DIED LAUGHING

One of my elderly lady friends was acutely aware of her sins and weaknesses and she tried to make amends where she could. I asked her once what her biggest regret was. Without even pausing to think about it, she said, "Being a smart aleck! I have always told people exactly what I think. I have been outspoken all my life. I was too hard on people."

Sometimes, she could even be a little proud of her tough side. On day, in one of her three nursing homes (I forget which one) I said to her, "Everyone around here knows you're strong willed." She smiled and said gleefully, "I do have some of them intimidated, don't I?" On another occasion, she had called her doctor a "goon." When I said it was not nice to call people "goons," she said, "I know, but I enjoyed it." Another time I said to her, "You're a little hard-headed, aren't you?" She smiled back at me and said these prophetic words, "Someday you'll stand over my dead body and say, "Now there's a woman who ran her own life." Once, after she had fallen twice without breaking any bones, I said to her, "You're a tough old lady, aren't you?" to which she responded, "I've been tough all my life. I've had to do what I had to do!"

Sometimes she would get confused and know she was confused. One such day, she leaned forward and asked, "What's it like going around with someone who is losing her mind?" When I tried to assure her that she wasn't going crazy, she responded, "That's too bad. I sort of like being crazy!" She even dragged me into it one day when she asked me head on, "What if one of us gets dementia?" to which I said, "And which one of us do you think that will be?"

I thank God for her sense of humor. We laughed our heads off sometimes. One day in October of 2003, she said to me out of nowhere, "I never was a pretty child."

When I answered, "Me neither." we both laughed hysterically. On another occasion, I said something about me being fat. She looked at me right in the eyes and said, "You're not fat. (pause) Maybe a little plump, but certainly not fat."

At one point, she was calling me as many as eight times a day. When I pointed it out to her, she answered sheepishly, "I decided not to call anymore, but my finger would not cooperate!" When she did it again, only this time it was ten times a day, I got onto her about filling up my answering machine without leaving any messages. She said, "I knew you'd be mad, but I thought it would be worth it. I just wanted to hear your voice." One day, we were sitting in the lobby drinking coffee. She said to me, "They have some pretty girls working here, don't they?" I responded, "Yes, I guess so." She snapped back, "Ha! I thought so! I saw you looking!" Another time, I said to her, "How do you like my beard?" She responded with a smirk, "Fine. How do you like mine?" One morning, we were drinking coffee. She looked up and said, "Well, look at you, sitting there looking so cute." When I said back, "I think you're eyes are failing," she shot back, "Let 'em fail!" Funniest of all, I was telling her what I was going to say at her funeral. She listened carefully and then said, "Well, Father Knott, I hope you live long enough to be there." Not long before she passed, when she could not even speak, I left her room realizing that we had been laughing even while she was dying.

AN OLD LADY MAGNET

Let me be perfectly honest with you. I am a self-confessed old lady magnet. Elderly ladies latch on to me like white on rice. I know I have never been "cute," so it must be something else. Maybe I come across as a pathetic abandoned puppy, a stranded cat, a crippled bird or something of that nature?

It is so bad that I remember telling Archbishop Kelly when we were house mates at the Cathedral Rectory, that one of my elderly lady friends had died that day. His response was immediate. He didn't bat an eye. He shot back, "I'm not worried. You'll have another one by 5:00!"

Well he wasn't far off. A few days after the funeral of another lady friend, Marea Gardner, one of the aged ladies of the parish called me. Barely back from the cemetery, my phone rang. The voice said, "I hear there's an opening!"

I have pledged to quit being so charming to elderly ladies. For the last 35 years I have been burning up the highways going to nursing homes every week. One case, in particular, comes to mind. When I was pastor of the Cathedral, I was asked to go visit an older woman. I was told she was very sick, close to death and had no relatives. (If someone ever tells you that, don't believe them. It's a trap!) Well, being new to Louisville, I fell for it - hook, line and sinker. I naively went to see her. She was a wonderful and charming woman, so it did not take her long to sink her hooks into me. Once she set the hook, I could not escape. After two or three trips, I knew it was going to be another case of "until death do us part."

One thing you need to know is, that if you go once, they are like drug addicts. You can't stop until one of you is dead. Well, in her case, she did not die as "soon" as I was led to believe. I made 525 trips to the nursing home over the next ten years. I thought that woman would never die.

Sometimes, these ladies don't come onto my radar one at a time. Sometimes they overlap, in layers, two or three or four deep – as was the case with Patricia Kirchdorfer. Patricia was a friend of Marea Gardner. I had been taking communion to Marea for a couple of years. At the beginning, Patricia was still driving herself to church. They lived in the same neighborhood. Well, as fate would have it, Patricia had to quit driving and then it started. "Me too! Me too! Since you're going to be in the neighborhood, how about bringing me communion on your way to Marea's house?" Well, it didn't take long before the hook was set. I estimate, between her house and the Episcopal Church Home, I made 300-400 communion calls, minimally, in the last few years. In fact, my car knows the way by itself.

Seriously, however, I am going to miss her. Like several of the others, we had many good laughs and happy moments together. Like Marea Gardner, Patricia had many interesting life experiences, was well read and had traveled extensively, so our visits were never boring. We could talk about a lot more than medications, walkers and hip replacements. She is going to leave a big hole in my life.

Now before any of you ladies get any bright ideas, know this. I am changing my phone number.

GRANDMA, PLEASE FIND ANOTHER JOB!

A friend of mine won a cruise at his health club. He couldn't find anyone to go with him, so I agreed. We flew into Miami, but the cruise left from Fort Lauderdale so we rented a car. It was late morning when we picked up the car and started driving toward the place we were to meet the ship. I was starving, but we needed to get there "soon." Somewhere along the way, I spotted a concrete block building surrounded by pick-up trucks with a huge sign that said "Doughnuts." It was an odd building, I thought, for a doughnut shop, but we were in a hurry. When we opened the door, we found ourselves in a long back-and-forth line leading up to a hostess who was seating people. You could not tell much about the place behind all the men in line. With all the trucks outside, I though it was just a favorite for guys going to work. It wasn't until we made the last turn in the line did we realize that it was a "topless doughnut shop." There were rails between the line posts keeping the line straight, so we could not get out of line, only go forward.

My friend suggested that we go somewhere else. I resisted saying we did not have time to go somewhere else. I was so hungry that I was determined to get a lemon filled doughnut to go. The topless hostess seated us. I ordered two lemon doughnuts to go. We left in a hurry.

What was the whole experience like? Well, if you can imagine your topless grandmother serving you breakfast, then you pretty well get the picture!

GOD AND CHEAP CIGARS

It was during my years at Saint Peter Mission Church in Monticello that I had a significant Saint Paul type conversion experience. It happened in a dream, a very vivid, memorable and life-changing dream. In the dream I was on top of a small mountain. It had no trees or bushes or rocks. It had only very short green grass like a golf green. I was sitting in a folding lawn chair and God was sitting in one next to me. We were sitting side-by-side facing the setting sun without speaking. We were both smoking cheap King Edward cigars! I knew it was God, but I was afraid to look over. We just puffed on our cigars and watched the sun set on the horizon. Finally, God leaned over and whispered in my ear, "Ron, isn't this wonderful!" I woke from the dream at that point and the world looked forever different to me. All of the emotional chains that were holding me back had melted away. I felt a lightness in my heart that I had never felt before. It was OK to be me. I fully understood what it meant to be "created in the image and likeness of God." I was that lost sheep that Jesus embraced. I was the prodigal son who made it home to an unexpected warm welcome. I felt that I could succeed and do some good things. For the first time in my life I felt that I was good enough for God just the way I was. This experience was the beginning of a new way of preaching. Instead of looking for sins to condemn, I started looking for goodness to affirm. I believe that the years following the dream prepared me to offer a clear message of "good news" that appealed to so many alienated Catholics which led to the rapid and consistent growth of the Cathedral parish a few years later.

THE NOT-SO-GOOD SAMARITAN

When I celebrated my 25th anniversary of ordination to the priesthood in 1995, I was able to take my dream vacation – a cruise through the Greek islands. On the flight from New York to Athens, I took off my only pair of glasses and laid them on my lap and fell asleep. When I woke up, I had wallowed on them to the point they were just one big twisted ball of wire and glass. I couldn't see much, especially when it came to reading.

We ended up in Athens on Friday and started looking for a place to get my glasses fixed. We were standing on a street corner looking through a phone book for a place to get the frames repaired when a man approached and asked us whether we needed help. Little did we know that he was always on the alert to see if any tourists needed "help."

We told him we were looking for a place to get my glasses fixed. He immediately said, "Follow me. It's just down this street." Sure enough, the man behind the counter took my glasses and promised to have them ready on Monday. I was ecstatic because I thought I would have to go through the whole upcoming trip practically blind.

The man who helped us suggested that we buy him a drink at a bar "just down the street." It sounded like a reasonable way to show our thanks. He took us to the bar and seated us on the bar stools, but then disappeared even though he seemed to know everyone in the place.

In a minute or two, two sleazy looking women took their seats on each side of us, got very friendly and ordered drinks right with us! It did not take us long to come to the conclusion that we were set up with two hookers and our "helpful friend" was in on the whole deal. Trying to find a graceful way out, my friend stupidly said, "We are priests." They responded, "So? We don't care if you don't care." I quickly asked for the tab (over $100) and ran for the door. I learned that day that one can be blind in more than one way.

After being led by the hand and having menus read to me, I retrieved my glasses on Monday and had the best vacation of my life once we got on the boat.

IT'S HELL GETTING THERE AND BACK

I have led well over one hundred priest retreats in Canada, United States, the British Isles, the Bahamas and the Caribbean. When people hear that I "get to fly to so many places," many respond with "it must be nice" when a more appropriate response might be "that sounds like hell."

Anyone who thinks that frequent air travel is some sort of enjoyable experience has not done much flying, at least not to destinations far from home where you are making multiple connections. As you know there are constant delays. And heaven forbid you have a flight when bad weather moves in. Getting to pleasant destinations is often not worth the hassles of getting there and back. I have developed a real aversion to airplanes and airports – and it seems to be getting worse. Take, for example, my last trip which is somewhat typical of my experiences.

Last spring, I made it home safely from trip #10 to St.Vincent. For that trip I went through 14 airports - seven each way: Louisville, Miami, Bridgetown (Barbados), Bequia, Canouan, Union and Saint Vincent. Coming home, I was in all seven in reverse.

Going down on American Airlines, we were delayed in Miami for three hours for God-knows-what. I barely made my connection to my SVG Airlines flight to Saint Vincent from Barbados.

Coming home, we were stuck on the tarmac in Miami for two hours after we landed. This resulted in a frantic race through customs and the huge airport looking for the gate to Louisville which was at the end of a maze of elevators, trains and closed gates in a building labeled as "an addition." Even with the running, I made it just in time to board for Louisville. If that flight had not been delayed as well, I would not have made it home that night. So, getting home at 2:00 in the morning I felt "lucky."

If you think traveling down there is all about sunny beaches, luxury hotels and wonderful plane rides, think again! Traveling is usually two days of endless stress, heat, frustration and discomfort. I sometimes wonder why I do it and how long I will be able to do it! I hope God gives me the strength and patience to keep it up! I need God's help because, at 74, I do not have the stamina I used to have and I have never been that patient anyway!

MY FIRST CONFESSION

My First Confession as a child was a disaster. Sister Mary Ancilla took our class to church beforehand to check out the confession box for a practice run. I missed the practice for some unremembered reason, so when my turn came to enter the confession box on the "big day," it was a total mystery to me. It was small, like a telephone booth, and it was dark. The confessional had two sides for maximum efficiency. The priest opened a small window on one side and heard a confession, while the next sinner entered and got settled on the other. In those days, many people went to confession weekly, so the lines were often long. With only one priest in the parish hearing all those confessions there was no time to dally. There was a shelf for adults to lean their elbows on as they whispered their sins to the priest through the small window covered with a thin cloth. That shelf for leaning on was over my little head, so I did not see the door open. I heard the priest say, "OK, you can begin." but I could not figure where the voice was coming from, so I said nothing. I heard the window slide open and close several times before I finally noticed a glimmer of light coming through a hole around the radiator pipe running along the floor. What did I do? In desperation, I got down on the floor and put my little lips as close to the hole as I could and gave my confession on my hands and knees! I knew something was not right, but I couldn't figure out what, until some of the other kids said something about the "little window" as they shared their experiences. It was not until I said, "What window?" that I realized my embarrassing mistake. I didn't tell anybody: not the other kids, not Sister Mary Ancilla and certainly not Father Johnson. It was my little secret for many, many years.

BAD BACK

When I was a deacon at Saint Meinrad Seminary, we used to go out for "ministry assignments" maybe once a week. I remember going to a nursing home in Tell City near the seminary. I remember one incident in particular. I was walking down the hallway going somewhere, when an elderly lady in one of he rooms caught my eye. She was waving wildly for me to come into her room. I stopped and went back to see what she wanted. When I got up to her bedside, she asked me in an obvious seductive tone of voice, "Are you married?" I responded back telling her that I was studying to be a priest and that priest do not marry. She looked puzzled and said, "So you're not married?" "No, I am not." She huffed indignantly, "Well, don't look at me. I've got a bad back!" I thought I'd never quit laughing as I walked out of the room.

NO ONE HAS EVER TALKED THAT NICE TO ME!

Let me change a few details to protect the seal of confession. One day an old man on a walker came to confession. It took him and his son several minutes to get him into the confession box. Once in, he began by telling me that he was dying and that he needed to go to confession, but he could not bring himself to tell me what had been bothering him for the last fifty years. He said, "If I die with this sin on my soul, I will go to hell!" The problem was, he was too embarrassed to tell a priest what he had done all those years earlier and he felt that he had made "hundreds of bad confessions and communions" which he considered additional mortal sins as well.

To comfort him, I said, "Let me guess. When I get to the sin you stop me." I guessed it on the third or fourth try. I assured him that it was more common than he imagined and that he did not invent it. I assured him of God's forgiveness and told him it saddened me that he had worried himself sick all those years. When he left, he said to me, "Nobody has ever talked to me that nice in my life. Thank you, Father."

His son told me months later that his father had died. He also said to me, "I don't know what he told you and I don't know what you told him, but he came out of that box with a grin on his face and told me he was ready to die. He never stopped smiling until he passed."

FANTASY LAND: TV SHOWS ABOUT PRIESTS

Television never gets it right. Priests always seem to come off these days as pious, angry or creepy. There are many very fine priests in this country who serve their people selflessly. Many are pastoring multiple parishes. Sadly, there are no made-for-TV "specials" about them and their work.

In the last several years, I have had the opportunity to listen to hundreds and hundreds of these priests from every part of the country. Most of our time was spent discussing very serious issues facing priests, but we did seem to make room for a good time. In fact, we could even laugh at ourselves.

In that vein, a few months back I started thinking about some possible new "priest shows" for television. Here goes:

I Love Loosey: An outrageous comedy about two liberal young priests in the 1960s ministering in a bilingual southern California parish. There's nothing they won't change.

Law and Order: A dull and tedious police series about young "neocons" on a mission to "save" the church.

Friday Night Smackdown: Liberal and conservative priests take each other on in no-holds-barred, hand-to-hand combat. Screaming parishioners back their favorite priests and often enter the ring themselves to avenge dirty tactics.

Elim-A-Priest: In an alternative to traditional personnel boards, parishes bid on new pastors after going out to eat with them a few times. Various priests with serious personality defects and obnoxious personal habits are "weeded out," while one single "Perfect Pastor" is hired at the conclusion of each show.

Father Emeril: A cooking show featuring various "rectory cuisines" for the stressed out and overworked, twinned and clustered parish priest. Heavy on Crock Pot, Seal-A-Meal and George Foreman Grill recipes from his new cookbook, "Cooking After Your Bypass Surgery."

Extreme Father Make-Over: This new show would be a wildly popular weekly series where pot-bellied, unkempt priests are nominated by their parishioners for liposuction, tummy tucks, Botox, unwanted hair removal and wardrobe updates. Parishioners shriek in approval when "Father-What-A-Waist" is turned into "Father-What-A-Waste."

Neo-Archaeology: Teams of young priests dig through rectory attics and parish sacristies in search of perfectly preserved birettas, copes, cassocks, fiddle-back vestments and other "precious artifacts" of the pre-Vatican II church, rescuing them "before it's too late."

Home Alone: This latest "reality show" features various priests living alone in big, empty rectories on Friday and Saturday nights while playing Solitaire and "voting themselves off the island" for entertainment. Boring!

Little Rectory on the Prairie: The Vatican, in a secret experiment, assigns a married priest to live in one of the secluded parishes of some unnamed Minnesota diocese. After the priest's wife gives birth to an obnoxiously sweet daughter, Laura, and after they almost starve to death on a priest's salary, the Vatican decides to cancel the experiment and declares the idea of married priests "unworkable."

Golden Boys: Four retired priests move into a condo together in some unnamed Florida diocese. This may be one of the dullest shows to ever be put on TV.

MATCHMAKER

A few years back, after slaving over a hot altar all day, I dragged myself home about 9:30 at night. On the way in the door, I picked up the mail – just a single strange looking envelope. I dropped my bulging briefcases on the floor, slumped down on the couch and looked at the envelope. It was from "Matchmaker International" and it was addressed to "occupant." Down in the corner was a lavender heart over-laid with the words "special offer for select singles."

My hands trembled as I opened the envelope. "Dear single friend," it said, "A more active and fulfilling social life could be days away. No longer does single mean being alone." At the bottom of the letter, it instructed me to turn the page for my "preliminary compatibility questionnaire." With tears of laughter running down my cheeks, I obeyed. "Which of the following," it asked, "makes it difficult for you to meet people? Check all that apply."

I had to choose between the following five categories.

(1) I meet enough people, but they are not my type. (I am pretty picky so I gave that one a checkmark.)

(2) My job makes it difficult or impossible to meet the right person. (I gave that one ten check marks and an Amen!)

(3) I don't feel comfortable asking someone for a date. (Check. Check. Check.)

(4) I am a single parent. (Here I wrote "I'm not sure" just for the hell of it.)

(5) I am already in a relationship of convenience. (I wonder what they meant by
“ convenience?”)

Next, it asked me to list three interests or activities that I would most like to share with a friend or partner. At this point I was cry-laughing so hard that I had to stop. After finishing off a five-pound bag of M&Ms, I decided to tear the questionnaire up and go to bed.

THE SHOW MUST GO ON

Around 2015, I agreed to do a Parish Mission at Saint Joseph Church in Butchertown. It was to be three weekday nights in row. The week came for the Parish Mission and I was bedridden with the flu, but it was not possible to cancel because it had been advertised quite well. On top of being sick, the city was blanketed with snow and ice. I had no choice other than to get out of bed, take a shower and head downtown even though I had been vomiting all day and I had a bad case of diarrhea.

Each night, I took a gallon size zip lock plastic bag and placed it in the pulpit and a change of underwear and an extra pair of trousers for the sacristy – just in case!

I made it to the last night without incident. Right before the final blessing, I pulled out the plastic bag and held it up for the congregation to see and told them about my emergency change of clothes in the sacristy. To my surprise, no one even suspected that I was sick.

THE SOUP'S ON!

My first day in first grade, Sister Mary Ancilla had to help us navigate the cafeteria at lunch time – balance a tray with food on it and carry it to the table. That day we had vegetable soup, a corn muffin and a small carton of milk. I took a tray and shuffled through the line as the cafeteria lady put a muffin on it and then a bowl of soup. Well, my muffin rolled off onto the floor. Sister Mary Ancilla dutifully bent down to pick it up. As she did, I watched her instead of focusing on balancing my tray. As a result, the bowl of soup slid off and hit her on her head. She was wearing a very starched bonnet like all Sisters of Charity did in those days. The warm soup "melted" her starched bonnet and it sort of drooped around her neck to the point her hair was showing – close to a mortal sin back then! She ran out of the cafeteria and up the steps to her room to change into another before most of the kids could see her and start laughing. Before she died in her nineties, I think I reminded her of it at least fifty times. We would both laugh every single time.

LITURGICAL LUNACY

When I was Vocation Director, I had a plan that I would visit every parish in the Archdiocese to talk about vocations, especially to priesthood and religious life.

One of the downsides of my plan was the fact that I did not plan on seeing some of the dumbest liturgical practices imaginable. That's why I always said that, at the

Cathedral, we were simply going to "do what's in the book well." Instead of "creativity," we were going to focus on "quality."

In one parish, they had the practice of the priest going to communion after the congregation had been served. Well, after giving out communion, I went directly to my chair as usual instead of going over to the credence table to take communion. It was not until I was walking down the aisle during the closing hymn that I realized that I did not go to communion at all during that Mass. The next Mass, I followed the rubrics of the church, not some local amateur liturgists idea of clerical humility.

In another parish, I went to my place in the sanctuary for the opening hymn, the penitential rite and the opening prayer. I had a sense that something was wrong, but it was not until I got ready to sit down that I noticed there was no chair. As I looked around totally confused, I asked the server, "Where is my chair?" He whispered, "Father always sits in the second pew!" Some amateur liturgists strike again!

Homemade communion bread! I never minded it much until I found out that many people know nothing about making it. At one Mass, there was a large disc that looked like pressed sawdust. It fell apart in thousands of small pieces when I tried to pick it up! In another parish, their homemade bread looked fine, but when I broke it in preparation for communion, I discovered it was raw inside. The gooey center stretched like a huge rubber band. I did not know what to do with it. Do I have to eat it? Do I go ahead and give it to people and hope they don't notice that it was mostly raw dough? Do I put Jesus back in the oven and continue baking him?

Homemade vestments! Now here is a world you do not want to enter. I have worn more, unnaturally colored, ugly double knit monstrosities in my day than all my aunts and sisters ever did in the 1970s! Some had kids' handprints stamped all over them. Others had ridiculous slogans. Others had grape leaves and wheat shafts. Still others looked like homemade political signs. By far the worst was a chasuble that had been made for a military chaplain out of a parachute. That priest insisted that I could "wear his special chasuble," as if it were some valuable antique worn by several Popes in the Middle Ages. I resisted. He insisted. I put it on and started up the aisle. Made out of very thin material, I am sure I looked like I was wearing a fairy costume in a school play. I could not wait to take it off after Mass.

Somebody needs to open a "Tacky Liturgical Museum" and collect some of these "art pieces" before they disappear, never to be seen again. I remember seeing a purple polka-dotted ceramic chalice in the Cathedral safe when I arrived there. If I had not thrown it way, it would should have had a "pride of place" in that new museum.

BACKPACKING IN EUROPE

In the first six years of priesthood, I made five back packing trips to Taize, France, to meet up with 3,500 students each week from all over the world. It was sort of a week-long religious Woodstock. After the week-long retreat, we would camp out in several countries until we made our way back to the airport in Paris.

I am still in contact with a few of the European students I met back then. I always took students from Somerset Community College with me to Taize. I have so many memories of those trips. Here are a sample.

One day we were coming out of Amsterdam, in the Netherlands, headed toward Germany to meet up with some friends. Amsterdam was known all over the world as a place floating in drugs. We were crossing the border in some small remote crossing. We had a car full of students. We looked suspicious to the local border guards, so they pulled us over for a total search – the car and each one of us personally. They searched every inch of the car. We were asked to strip so they could search us as well.

It did not take them long to find our little stash of pills that Dr. Weigel of Somerset gave us for nausea, diarrhea and headaches. The guards were convinced that they had uncovered a stash of illegal drugs. Since it was a minor border crossing, all they had was a small test kit. They tested each pill until all of a sudden one of them "tested for cocaine." We all panicked, convinced that we were going to be "locked up abroad."

Not trusting their test kit, they sent it all to the nearest town while we waited several hours for the results. When the results came back, they realized it was a mistake and what we had was harmless. They gave our medicine back to us and sent us on our way. I was so shaken by the incident that, when we got out of sight, I started throwing pills out of the window until they were all gone. I didn't want to go through that again!

One night, in Switzerland, we parked our rented car in an apple orchard, off the road a bit, to spend the night sleeping on the ground. About an hour after going to sleep I was awakened by a slow creeping sound that I could not identify. I sat up and realized that a slow moving car, with its lights on, had just missed my head.

One day, I had two students from Somerset (Joe and Larry) in the car with me as I was driving through Switzerland. I had made several trips to Europe by that time, so I knew pretty much how things worked. This gave me a chance to pull a few fast ones on them.

At one point, Joe (who is now a successful doctor) was in the back seat reading a book. Cows were grazing on a steep slopes on each side of the road, so I said to Joe, "Have you noticed that cows in Switzerland have two short legs and two long legs so they can stand on the sides of mountain?" He rose from his book reading, yelling, "Really? Really? Where are they?" Larry and I laughed our heads off. Realizing he had been made a fool of, Joe barely spoke to me the rest of the day.

Father David Stoltz, a fellow diocesan priest, was with me on one of my Taize trips, when we drove down to Rome to see the Vatican and Saint Peter's Basilica.

At one point, we were inside Saint Peter's Basilica, probably one of the most sacred churches in all of the Catholic world. We sat down on the steps of the high altar under the famous Bernini columns, over on the right side.

I was going on and on about how many Popes and Kings had climbed the steps we were sitting on and how the walls were saturated with the prayers of millions and millions of people. I talked about the Pieta by Michelangelo and the body of St. Pius the X and Popes I never heard of.

After about fifteen minutes of my pious lecturing, Father David passed gas so loudly you could hear it echoing off the dome! I was embarrassed and grossed out but also trying to hold back raucous laughter. I ran laughing to some secret corner hoping not to be noticed. David loved to stick a pin into sacred balloons. That had to be one of his best efforts!

On another trip, we met a couple of students from Scotland going north to Germany. It was raining one night so the four of us would not be able to sleep in our small car. Derek, one of the Scots, insisted that he could sleep in the trunk. I did not think it was a good idea, but I was willing to let him try it until he begged to be let out.

We put him in his sleeping bag and lifted him into the trunk and shut the lid. Well, several hours went by and I was awakened by a scratching sound coming from the trunk. I was convinced that gas fumes had overcome him and his scratching was his last effort to get help.

Scared to death, we all got out of the car, opened the trunk and there he was grinning up at us. He had been eating some green apples that he had in his backpack. That explained the crunching/scratching noise. We slammed the trunk door and we all went back to sleep, knowing he would be OK.

On another trip, we drove to eastern Austria to a farm where one of our Taize acquaintances lived. He invited us to visit. It was like going back to World War I Europe. The grandmother was baking bread in a brick hearth when we arrived. The living room was lit by a bare bulb hanging in the center of the room.

The house was built in a square with a courtyard in the middle, where the cows were brought in for the night to be milked and bedded down. To get to the bathroom (an outhouse really) in the middle of the night, you had to find your way through the cows to the door of the outhouse. As nature would have it, I had to go about 3:00 in the morning. I can still remember feeling my way though the cows in the dark to where the outhouse was, find the door knob, do my business and feel my way back through the cows back to my bed. The smell of manure permeated the house, so some more on my shoes was not a problem.

The next morning, I awoke to the sound of giggling children sitting in the window sill staring at me sleeping. It seemed that the kids had rounded up their friends from the neighborhood to see the visiting "Americans."

I still remember the huge loaves of freshly baked bread and the freshly churned butter and newly laid eggs we had for breakfast that morning! It was sooooo good!

RECTORY COOKS

The first time I experienced having a rectory cook who looked after the needs of the priests living in the rectory was when I was a transitional deacon in my last semester of my seminary years. In the parish I was assigned to, there were four of us, but not so much these days when priests tend to live alone.

The cooks tended to have a lot of control over what you ate, when you ate and how much you ate. They had a lot of control. They were sometimes more like an irritated stepmother than a church employee.

I tried to follow the local customs in how to relate to the cook at that parish, but one day I committed a "mortal sin" in her eyes and she flew into an angry harangue. I was caught eating a banana after supper. She saw it and let me know in no uncertain terms that "the bananas are for breakfast!" Not to be outdone, I responded in a very calm voice. "I know. I'm just having my breakfast tonight. I like to eat it before I go to bed. It saves me a lot of time in the morning." My response left her speechless. She just stood there for a moment, turned on her heels and went back into the kitchen without ever mentioning bananas ever again. To this day, when I see a banana, I often think of her.

BEARD REACTIONS

I had a full beard for my first 25 years of priesthood. I grew it during my first trip to Taize, France, in 1971. On my 25th anniversary as a priest, I shaved it down to a smaller Van Dyke.

I was serving as associate pastor of Saint Mildred Church in Somerset, Kentucky, when I first grew my beard. When I came home from Taize, I remember being a bit apprehensive about how it might be viewed by the congregation – so apprehensive that I basically stayed out of sight until I walked up the aisle for Mass the weekend I got home. I remember hearing some mild gasps as they realized what I had on my face.

After Mass, as I was standing out front of the church, I overheard two older ladies discussing my beard. One said in my defense, "Saint Francis had a beard." The other lady responded with a huff, "Well, he isn't Saint Francis!"

By the time I retired, my Van Dyke had turned snow white, so I decided to shave it all off. This caused me to have to change my photo for my column in *The Record*. This left me clean shaven for the first time since I was ordained. As I was backing out of the garage one day, one of the neighbor ladies got me attention. I rolled down the window to speak to her. "I like your new photo in *The Record*. You don't look like a gangster." A gangster? I didn't know whether to thank her or run over her.

NOT OVER RATED, FOR SURE – PART ONE

At one of the receptions after my First Mass, a young woman came up to me and asked me how long I went to school. I answered her, "Well, counting grade school, I went to school for twenty years."

She gasped, took a step backwards and said, "My God, you could have been something!"

I learned early in my priesthood that (1) some people do not value my vocation as much as I do (2) some people will put into words about anything that comes into their minds (3) I have a tendency to remember "put downs" even if they are not meant to be "put downs" and (4) they end up becoming occasions of laughter later in life.

NOT OVER RATED, FOR SURE – PART TWO

My former neighbor was a member of the Church of Christ and had a beehive hairdo. She was a very sweet lady who always greeted me with a smile. She had a daughter-in-law who was a Catholic. She always spoke of her daughter-in-law as if her Catholicism was an inherited affliction she could not help, but whom she loved anyway. I don't think she ever understood her bias and she certainly would never do anything consciously to hurt anyone's feelings, including mine.

Her Catholic daughter-in-law gave her a copy of one of my books one Christmas. When I ran into her a few weeks after she said to me, "My daughter-in-law gave me a copy of your new book for Christmas. I loved it. I had no idea you were that smart!" She smiled at me as if she had given me her best compliment. I smiled back, knowing she meant well, but went to my condo, shut the door and laughed my head off.

NOT OVER RATED, FOR SURE – PART THREE

When I went to Saint Peter Mission Church to be the first Catholic priest to live in Wayne County, Kentucky, one of the first things I had to do was to raise my own salary. There were only eight parishioners and five of them were children.

I held a meeting with the parishioners to brainstorm ideas about how to fund myself. I was thinking in terms of maybe getting a teaching job or working in a social service agency or maybe asking some parishes in Louisville to support me.

Not too long into the brainstorming session, the oldest parishioner who had recently become Catholic after her Catholic husband had died, raised her hand, "I hear they are looking for young guys to bag groceries down at the Pic Pac market." I was stunned, but tried not to show it. I had just finished twenty years of formal education and she wants me to be a bag boy at a grocery store? It was a quick lesson in humility that came in handy in the subsequent years.

One of the routine questions I was asked, when people found out I was a "preacher" was, "Did you go to school?" At first, I was beginning to think I looked stupid or something. No, it was because there were two classes of ministers – those with an education who were "called" by their denomination and those without formal education who were "called" by God directly. They tended not to trust "educated" preachers.

ONE FLU OVER THE CUCKOO'S NEST

Last fall, I made a trip to Calgary in Alberta, Canada, for a deacon retreat followed by a priest retreat.

Besides the largest one-day snowfall in Calgary for 104 years, I was put in a room at an old convent novitiate with a heating system in need of repair. It was so hot in the room, with no way to regulate the temperature, that I had to open the window and let in a stream of arctic air to be able to breathe. This led to my getting a terrible cold. Besides that, the wi-fi in the retreat center was down for the weekend, so to be able to communicate with the outside world via the internet, I had to walk several blocks to a coffee shop. However, the deacon retreat went well.

On Monday, we drove up to Banff for the week-long priest retreat. All week I was sneezing and blowing my nose. By the end of the retreat, I knew I was coming down with the flu – even though I had received my flu shot a few weeks before. In the car on the way back to Calgary, I thought about my passport. I assumed that it was in the pocket of the pants I wore coming up to Canada and I would check on it as soon as we got back to Calgary.

By the time we got back to Calgary where I would spend the night in the Cathedral rectory, I was really feeling badly. I went to bed right away, with chills that made my teeth chatter. I was throwing up as well. In the middle of this, I remembered my passport. I checked my pants pocket and everything in my suitcase. It was not there. I began to panic. The bishop was still there in the rectory, so he and the pastor began to think of ways I could check everywhere I had been that week. It could have meant checking the hotel in Banff, an hour and a half away. We even began to look for the United States embassy in Calgary in case we might need to request a duplicate of my passport – which could take days.

I called the coffee shop where I had gone for wi-fi several times during the deacon retreat. Then I called the retreat house to see if anyone had turned in my passport. No one had, but they said they would check the room I stayed in. By this time, I was in a panic for sure. In a few minutes, the retreat house called back and said that they had found it under the bed. Evidently, it had fallen out of my pants pocket when I was folding them and bounced under the bed. I was so relieved.

I went back to bed, but there was a meeting next door with loud voices that lasted over four hours. At this point, I was ready to move. I asked the pastor to call a cab and make reservations at an airport hotel, using the excuse that "I could be at the airport in the morning for my trip home." I got to the hotel at 6:00 pm and slept until 11:00 am the next day. I flew home at 1:00 pm.

I was so sick and disoriented at the airport that I dropped my billfold coming through security. Someone ran up to me to give it back. When I put my passport into the machine to go through customs, I walked away and left it there. Someone else found it and ran up to me to return it.

The plane had mechanical problems on the runway which delayed our departure. There were storms in Chicago which delayed our landing there. I finally got home at 1:00 in the morning. The next day I woke up with huge fever blisters from my upper lip to my nose. I was in bed for about ten days trying to recover. I did get out of bed for a wedding planning meeting and my home parish's 200th anniversary. There was one good thing to come out of this – I lost about six pounds.

I was so worn down by all this that I decide not to go to the islands before Christmas as I had planned, but to wait until February.

I have had many adventures similar to this over the last several years, including an overnight in Charlotte because of fog, snow storms in Ottawa, Canada, and Crookston, Minnesota, and a false test for explosives in Saint Lucia. If you don't laugh, you cry!

HITTING THE JACKPOT

Growing up, my father bought the old Saint Theresa Academy farm that surrounded the church property in Rhodelia, Kentucky. As a result, the whole area around he church became a playground of sorts for me and my brother, Gary. When we were not doing chores around the farm, we had time to explore the woods that embraced the church on almost every side.

When the old Academy building was razed, a lot of the junk went into a ravine below the church. People were not as conscious of the environment back then, so the ravine dump became one of the most interesting places to explore. It had all kinds of interesting stuff.

One day, my brother and I were going through the heap of junk when I came across a heart shaped vigil light stand from the church that Father Johnson had decided to discard. There used to be two matching ones in the sanctuary – one on each side of the church. I can still remember that familiar sound of quarters and nickels sliding down the metal slot as people came up to light candles. I suppose this stand was broken beyond repair or Father Johnson thought one was enough. Anyway, one of them made it to the dump.

When I saw the stand, I picked up a small stick of wood and gave it a whack. I am not sure why, but I did. When I hit it, the money chamber exploded like a slot machine at a casino. Nickels, dimes and quarters rolled out of it for what seemed forever. It amounted to a little over $25 – huge money in those days. It was so full of coins that it apparently didn't rattle which caused Father Johnson not to even check it before it went to the heap.

We gathered up the coins, put them in a small box and hid it in our garage while we tried to figure out what to do with the windfall. When you are a kid with no money, it takes time to think through such a moral dilemma.

Should we just spend it? I knew that in a small town like ours, if I showed up at the store every day with money in hand to buy candy and soft drinks it would have set off alarm bells. We knew we could not resist holding back from spending it for long so we rejected that option. I knew that Father Johnson would not have thrown it away if he knew it was filled with money, so my conscience got the best of me. I knew we had to take it back and hope against hope that he would say, "Finders keepers. Losers weepers!" We decided to return the money and keep our fingers crossed. Bad idea. He took the box of money and gave us a quarter each as a reward! I left there that day thinking to myself, "Crime may not pay, but neither does honesty." It was a hard lesson in morality.

CAUGHT AFTER ALL THOSE YEARS

I don't think I ever got away with much growing up, as far as my father was concerned. He seemed to have an ability to find out about every mistake I made. It seemed like he had eyes in the back of his head or I was living in a world of people willing to report every offense. However, one day I thought I had actually escaped blame for a major accident without even having to lie just by keeping my big mouth shut.

My Dad had a building material business which meant many trips to Louisville to pick up those supplies. When we would get home from school, my brother and I were always faced with a truck that needed to be unloaded: concrete blocks, lumber, dry wall, fertilizer and about anything needed to construct a building.

One day, I jumped up on the back of the loaded truck with a tarpaulin over it. I stood on the tarpaulin and heard on ominous cracking noise as I sank deeper and deeper. I realized right away that under that tarpaulin were about 12 glass storm doors! I freaked out, but said nothing. When my Dad came up to the truck, I uncovered the broken windows and let out a fake gasp. He saw the disaster and shouted,

"Damn it! I knew when I hit that pot hole on Dixie Highway something broke." I stood there looking very sympathetic at *his* mistake.

In a homily in Monticello one Sunday about twenty-five years later I recounted the episode. Well, as fate would have it, he later came for a Monticello visit one Sunday. As we were standing around after church, one of the ladies said to him, "I love that story he tells about the time he stepped on a tarpaulin covering a dozen storm doors and broke all of them."

She stood there and proved the point that I never got away with anything growing up. I only thought I did.

NIAGARA FALLS

When I was a deacon serving at Saint John Vianney parish, Father Harold Ritter was the pastor. He was getting up there in years and it was noticeable that he was "losing it" a little bit at a time. Cordless microphones were coming into use with the "new Mass" which was more interactive with the congregation. Many of us were not good at turning them on and off at the right time.

One Sunday, after a Mass that Father Ritter celebrated and I served as his deacon, I went to the back of the church to greet the people. Father Ritter made a mad rush to the toilet in the sacristy. As I was standing there talking to a group of people, it became obvious that Father Ritter had not turned off his microphone! Now wait - it's worse than you think.

I stood there speechless as his urination sounded like Niagara Falls coming over the sound system in the church. We all stood there looking at each other a little embarrassed as we realized what it was. Then all of a sudden, he passed gas, long and loud, and ended it with a long "aaah" of relief as the whole church burst out in laughter. I think someone even started to clap!

A CHAPEL BY ANY OTHER NAME

At one time I was part-owner of a vacation lake house with my friend, Tim Schoenbachler. There were several other priests who also had vacation houses on the same lake. Several of us priests would take the same day off and meet there on Tuesdays. The Ursuline Sisters also had a house there, left to them by a priest who had passed away.

The house that Tim and I owned had a bathroom on the front of the house facing the road. It had a tall and narrow clear window that did not afford any privacy, so Tim designed a panel of stained-glass that was set over it.

The Sisters down the road would often walk by our house. One day their curiosity about the stained-glass window got the best of them. They decided to stop in and ask about it. When I opened the door, one of them said, "Can we see your chapel, Father?" "The chapel?" I questioned. "Yes, we have noticed your beautiful stained-glass window and we want to see your chapel." Without even a hint of a smile, I took them back to the bathroom and opened the door. "Here is our chapel. I hope you like it!" There it was, shower on the left, toilet on the right and stained glass in the middle.

ARE YOU TAKING THIS SERIOUSLY, FATHER?

On my ordination day, I went to Churchill Downs and got there in time for second race. Yes, with chrism oil still wet on my anointed hands, I went to a race track!

I was working out of Saint John Vianney Parish near Churchill Downs when I was ordained a priest. I didn't have any family in town and all my friends were busy with their own festivities. I did not want to go down to my home parish and spend the night before my First Mass there the next day. As a result, I did not know what to do with myself after ordination. It wasn't like I was going on a honeymoon or anything of that nature. I decided to go to the track for the afternoon since it was so close by.

I intended to get there for all the races, but I was stopped in the parking lot at Saint John Vianney by a woman who wanted to go to confession. I first thought of referring her to a priest, but I remembered that I was now a priest. We went over to the church. She began by saying that it had been "fifty years" since her last confession. Hearing that I settled back because I knew I was going to be there a while. I don't know who was more nervous – her or me. All I knew was that I was missing the fist race.

SQUEEZING THE CHARMIN

Archbishop Kelly was a very patient man. He did not want special treatment in the rectory. When he needed something, he would leave me a hand-written note on the steps. I have kept many of them because they are so funny. Some I cannot include in this book.

One day he left me a note saying he was out of toilet paper. I told the housekeeper that Archbishop Kelley needed toilet paper. That night, he had a note on his steps from the housekeeper that said simply, "We don't have any." Most people would have screamed, "Well, go get some!" Instead, we both just laughed our heads off for the rest of the evening.

HOW ABOUT A REFUND?

For many years I lived across the street from an elderly German lady who eventually became an "adopted mother." She had no children of her own, so she insisted that I call her "Mama King."

I met her when I was a seminarian looking for a place to live in Louisville where I had a summer job at a nearby hospital. She and her husband rented a basement apartment to me. Whenever I had a holiday break from the seminary I stayed with them as well. After ordination, I bought a house near to them. She became my unpaid housekeeper. She had a key and would come in and leave things for me all the time.

One day I mentioned that it was so cold I was thinking about getting some flannel sheets. Well, I learned to be careful what I mentioned because she would go find it "on sale," of course.

I came home one night to find new flannel sheets on my bed. They had little teddy bears printed all over them. When she asked me how I liked them I told her they were fine but I was a bit embarrassed by the teddy bears. The sheets looked more like bed linens for a 3 year old. I underscored that they would be fine since no one would see them but me. I slept on them for about a week, laughing every night to myself when I got in bed.

Then one day, they were gone. When I asked her where they were, she said, "I washed them, folded them up nicely and took them back and got a refund." She would do things like that all the time. She had a way of brow beating reluctant sales people in the stores until she got what she wanted. There were many times I have walked out of stores and waited in the car when she was in one of her "refund" moods. She was a one-of-a-kind.

... AND THE WINNER IS!

The year after I left Holy Name of Mary Church in Calvary, I heard they were having their annual Halloween Party and Dance for adults, something I had started when I was there.

That year, a store where you could get Halloween costumes, was having a "buy a mask and get a free tuxedo rental" promotion. I could not resist. I bought a full mask that covered my whole head, front and back. It had long gray hair. With a tuxedo, tails and the mask, I looked like an orchestra conductor.

I decided to crash the Halloween Party without telling anyone who I was or that I was even coming. I came early and stayed late. I spent the whole evening interacting with my former parishioners without speaking of course. Absolutely no one suspected it was me and no one imagined it was a priest, so I heard many, many funny comments.

When it came time to announce the winner of the "best costume," I was totally surprised that I won first prize. With the whole room focused on me, I turned around and pulled off the mask. The whole room let out a scream of delight. They could not believe it. I was surprised that no one even suspected. One of the things I loved about that place is that we had so many good times together. That was just one of many.

NO BIG LOSS

I have owned a total of four houses on Eastern Parkway. In the first three, I had break-ins at least once. Before I moved into my present condo, someone broke into my house in the 900 block. The thieves broke out a back window after I went to work. All they took was a drawer of change I had in the bedroom. The police summarized that it was some teenagers looking for guns or money.

When I told Archbishop Kelly about it, he responded in his typical understated way, "Well isn't that pitiful? A break-in and they didn't see anything they wanted except a bag of pennies!"

A PET SITTING DISASTER

Some people, I am convinced, are not meant to own pets. I would include myself and one of my best friends from my seminary days.

My friend, Pat Murphy, decided to buy a parakeet after seeing an old bird cage at the Jasper, Indiana, Saint Vincent de Paul store where we were regular shoppers.

> I digress for a moment, but I once bought a small refrigerator there for \$20.00. It worked, but it had a homemade coat hanger hook to keep it shut. We were not allowed to have appliances in our rooms, but I decided to try to get it to my room unnoticed. I had it on the elevator headed to my room when the elevator stopped at the floor before mine. The elevator was small so, with the refrigerator and me, there was no room for anyone else. When the door opened, there stood the monk who was the supervisor of our floor. I kept my cool, shut the door and said I would send it back down shortly, with no explanation. It never occurred to him that I was taking it to my room, so he said nothing. I made history that day by becoming the first student to have his own refrigerator. I rented space to other students and, typical of my entrepreneurial ability, I sold it three years later at a profit!

Anyway, back to the parakeet. My friend, Pat, asked me to baby sit his new parakeet while he was gone for the weekend. I was to go to his room and check on its water and food. Well, he decided to give the parakeet a bath in the sink before he left. Whoever heard of such? If that was not bad enough, he put the wet bird and its cage on the radiator cover and opened the window a bit to give it air. Well, the heat came on at some point. The poor wet bird had arctic wind blowing over him and heat practically cooking him.

When I went to check on the poor parakeet, it was dead in the bottom of the cage with its feet in the air. I freaked out and tried to think of something to escape blame for not checking on it sooner. I finally drove to the pet store where he had purchased it with the intention of buying another to replace it and to say nothing. The pet store had another parakeet, but it was a totally different color. So I had to abandon plan A.

I decide to tell him the truth, but have the bird laid out in a nice little casket when he got home, thinking that might take out some of the sting of his loss. Well, before I knew it, everyone in the dorm knew about it. Just before Pat was to return they started dropping off little floral arrangements with messages of condolences. Before long the room was filling up and people were sitting around like it was a funeral home. When the door opened and Pat entered his room, everyone burst out into feigned weeping.

In the end, he took it better than I had imagined after we all had a good laugh. The next morning before class, we had a funeral procession down the hall, down two flights of stairs and out the door to a huge monument in the shape of a cross in front of the building. We buried it in front of the monument.

To this day, fifty years later, when I pass that huge cross, I look at the spot where we buried the parakeet and laugh to myself.

DOWN IN THE COUNTRY

From 1970 to 1983 I spent my ministry in the Kentucky missions in Somerset, Monticello and Whitley City and a rural parish in Calvary.

AN OVER-POPULATION PROBLEM

My very first assignment was Associate Pastor at Saint Mildred Church in Somerset, Kentucky, down on Lake Cumberland in south central Kentucky. Catholics were a minority in a very Baptist area of the state. Many people had never met a Catholic, much less a Catholic priest.

One of the benefits of that assignment was being able to go to the lake on Sunday afternoon to swim and cook out with some of the youth of the parish. On one such day, about a dozen young adults and I went on one of those Sunday afternoon trips.

We had our blankets spread out on the grass in a crowded picnic area. Our group was coming and going to the water, to the drink cooler and to the bathroom, inevitably yelling in my direction, “Father this and Father that!” Finally, a woman came over to me, obviously not familiar with possibility of a priest in her midst, asked in a serious tone of voice, “Sir! You look pretty young! Just how many kids do you have anyway?”

THE LONG HOT SUMMER

When I found out as a newly ordained priest that I would be going to Somerset, I freaked out on many levels. First, all throughout my seminary years, I was warned not to "screw up or they will send you to Somerset." It was known, unfairly, as a place where you were sent when they wanted you where you could do the least harm. Secondly, I knew Father Thomas Buren was pastor there. Father Buren was from my home parish. My father grew up with him. He warned me before I left that "the only way to get along with a Buren was to do it his way!" Father Buren was a "control freak," as we called people like that in the 1970s.

I overheard him on the phone one day talking to the diocesan personnel board. "When I said send me a young priest, I had no idea you would send somebody this young." He was talking about me, of course. Four months later they moved him and I stayed.

He would say things like this: "I am cooking tonight. You are welcome to join me if you like." I don't know where else he expected me to eat, but he wanted me to know that the rectory was his house and I was simply an imposed house guest.

He would not let me leave the rectory on Sundays "in case there was a sick call." The place was so dreaded by parishioners that I never heard the phone or doorbell ring. We both sat in our rooms all day. On top of that, my rooms had small windows above my eye sight. You had to stand on a chair or stool to see out. I lived that way for four long months, until he was transferred back to Louisville and Father Jerry Timmel arrived as the new pastor.

About the only time I got relief from his "prison guard behavior," was when he had to go on a trip for a few days. He left one Sunday night saying, "I'll be home Thursday." Well, this gave me a window of opportunity to have a little party in the rectory and invite some guys over to play poker on Wednesday night. The bourbon bottle was on the kitchen table and the poker game was in full swing when, all of a sudden, the back door opened and there stood Father Buren!

I let out a gasp and said, "I thought you said you'd be home Thursday." He replied in one of the coldest voices I have ever heard, "I said I would be home by Thursday." The party broke up before he had time to get to his room. He always did things like that in an attempt to catch you at something. I am going to be buried two graves down from him in our parish cemetery. I hope he leaves me alone.

JUST SAY "NO"

One day, in Somerset, I decided to try a new barber. As he was cutting my hair, and since he realized that I was not local, he began to ask me questions. I hesitated when he got to, "What do you do?" I knew that many people in that town had rarely met a Catholic and most had never met a priest. I did not want him to try to convert me, which some did. In his case, I decided to tell the truth to see what happened. "I'm a Catholic priest." There was a long pause before the next question. "Was your father a priest too?" Dreading a lengthy discussion on celibacy next, I simply answered, "No." We went on to another discussion.

CREMATION, ANYONE?

My first anointing of the sick took place at the old Somerset City Hospital in Somerset, Kentucky. I had only been ordained for a few weeks when I was called to anoint a dying woman. I grabbed the holy oil container from the parish office. When I arrived at the hospital, I was taken to an emergency room where she was in an oxygen tent. The nurses raised the plastic for me and I unscrewed the cap on the oil stock. All of a sudden, there was a blast of black powder, like a miniature explosion. I stood there in shock as I put the parts back together. Someone had filled the oil container with ashes from an Ash Wednesday service at one of the parish's mission churches in a Lent past. The pump on the oxygen tent pulled the ashes out of my little brass oil container and blew them all over her face and the pillow. All the wonderful Baptists standing around did not bat an eye. They all, no doubt, thought that it was part of the Catholics ritual we did at a time like that. Not to disappoint them, and to cover my mistake, I ended with a prayer that contained these words, “Remember, man, you are dust and into dust you shall return.” I left there and told no one, especially the pastor who had ordered me to go do the anointing in the first place.

LOSS OF APPETITE

When I was associate pastor of Saint Mildred Church and still living in the rectory in Somerset, I was living with the pastor, Jerry Timmel. Father Timmel was a hunter. He was proud of the fact that he could bring home wild animals for the rectory freezer to be dragged out for special occasions. He also liked to cook what he killed.

One night, I remember him standing at the freezer door looking at all the small frozen animal parts in plastic bags. He asked me, “What would you like for dinner tonight? Squirrel? Dove breasts? Venison? Rabbit?” I was a bit disgusted with the thought, so asked him back, “Got any hot dogs in there?” He answered back, “Sure! I bought some yesterday.” Well, besides being a hunter, he was “thrifty.” He always bought the cheapest of everything to save money.

I remember taking the package of hot dogs that looked sort of suspicious. It didn’t have a recognizable label. They were some sort of generic brand of hot dogs. I could not help reading the label. Under the ingredients, the first thing mentioned was “beef lips.” I thought I would lose it right then and there! “If beef lips were first in line, what on the other end of the cow might be in these hot dogs,” I thought to myself.

By this time, I had lost my appetite and decided to skip dinner. To this day, the thought of eating a hot dog makes me nauseous.

GETTING MARRIED? DON'T CALL ME!

In Somerset, I seemed to have more bad luck with weddings than anywhere.

I'LL NEVER FORGET OLD WHAT'S HER NAME?

One of the worst wedding mistakes I ever made taught me a good lesson. I had been friends with the groom and his old girlfriend, Theresa, for years. I was accustomed to using their names together. They broke up and the groom was about to marry his new girlfriend, Beth.

When we got to the wedding vows, I asked, "Joe, do you take Theresa to be your wife ... uh ... oh ... no!" The whole congregation laughed out loud since they knew exactly what I had done and why I had done it. The new bride even smiled, forgave me and the wedding went on. "Joe, do you take *Beth* to be your wife?"

It's always good to write names down in the ritual for weddings, baptisms and funerals, even if you think you can remember them!

SLIP N' SLIDE

Saint Mildred Church had a very slick terrazzo floor. There was a set of steps that led up to a small landing that was followed by another set of steps to a spacious sanctuary. The portable unfixed altar that was added after Vatican II stood between the two sets of steps on the small landing.

I was standing behind the moveable altar after the wedding as the bride and groom went behind me up to the sanctuary to light the "unity candles." As they made their way back down, the bride lost her balance on the steps and came crashing into me from behind. This pushed me and the moveable altar over the steps in front of me. She was literally on my back as I was holding onto the altar which had moved down one step.

There we were – priest, altar and bride all in a tangle, scared to move lest we come crashing down the other steps in a tangled ball. The ushers came forward to peel her off my back and push the altar back up the step so I could let go of it with breaking my neck in a fall. All's well that ends well!

THE DARN STEPS, AGAIN!

At another wedding in the same church with that slick terrazzo floor, I almost witnessed another fall.

In those days, leisure suits and platform shoes were stylish for men. The lector, after finishing his reading, started down the steps. Halfway down, his heel caught the edge of the steps and he went flying forward, gaining his balance at the very last moment, but not before letting out a loud "shit!" Even I had to laugh.

THE GONG SHOW

Before I knew I was not supposed to do it, I agreed to perform a civil ceremony for two of the students at Somerset Community College.

When I arrived for the backyard wedding, I noticed an arch with flowers at the end of the lawn where the wedding was to take place. They had even rented an organ and had it connected to an extension cord. The wedding cake was proudly displayed on a table in the nearby carport. The kitchen was full of food and there were tables set up across the lawn.

I got there a bit early to make sure I knew what was going to happen. By the time the wedding guests started to arrive, the weather was beginning to turn bad. Dark clouds hung ominously over the house. When the wedding was to begin, wind and rain had blown the floral arch to the ground, the rented organ was soaking wet and the top tier of the wedding cake had blown off and landed on the carport concrete.

We all moved inside. The wedding party squeezed into the living room. I was literally smashed against a grandfather clock that decided to chime at 11:00 o'clock in my right ear in what seemed like endless booms. I held up the ceremony until it stopped.

I was never so glad anything was over in my life! It was as if God was saying to me, "I told you that you were not supposed to do these kinds of weddings."

IF WE DON'T HAVE IT, WE CAN'T GIVE IT

When I was living in a basement apartment in Monticello, Kentucky, the first Catholic priest to reside in Wayne County, I was proud of the fact that we were able to establish a small social service ministry fund. In fact, we may have been the only church in the county to have such a fund to help people with their basic needs. We were so unique in this way that when I answered the phone one day, the person on the other end of the call asked, "Is this the church that helps people?" I remember chuckling to myself, "You mean the others don't?"

One day I got a call that went something like this. The caller stated, "I need to borrow some money." I answered politely, "Well, we try to help people whenever we can. What do you need?" He answered, "Well, I am thinking about building a carport for my car." I sounded shocked when I questioned him. "A carport? Sir, we can't help you with a carport. We only have $70.00 in the bank!" His response had an even more elevated tone of shock in it. "$70.00! Did you say $70.00?" After a somewhat stunned silence, he asked firmly, "Who is this?" I responded, "This is Father Knott. I am pastor here at Saint Peter Catholic Church." Obviously embarrassed, he half-way shouted before abruptly hanging up, "Well, hell, I thought I was talking to the Monticello Bank!"

THOSE FISH-EATING CATHOLICS!

Not too long after I moved in as the first resident pastor of Saint Peter Church in Monticello, I had a new sign built in front of the church. It featured the name SAINT PETER CATHOLIC CHURCH. Under the title of the parish, I put a large fish symbol – the one usually associated with Saint Peter, the fisherman, or the one that served as a secret symbol for early Christians – the ICHTHUS. The Greek letters of the word *ichthus* (fish) stands for the English words meaning, "Jesus Christ, Son of God, Savior" or "Jesus Christ, God's Son, Savior." This symbol was used primarily among Christians of the early church in the 1st and 2nd century A.D. The "fish" symbol was an identifying symbol Christians used to recognize each other.

I heard that the locals were telling people that it was a sign that Catholics ate a lot of fish, especially on Fridays! So much for ancient Christian symbols. We might as well have put a picture of a McDonald's Filet-of-Fish Sandwich under the words Saint Peter Catholic Church.

THAT OLD ADAMS FAMILY DOESN'T NEED OUR PRAYERS

When I was pastor of Saint Peter Church in Monticello, we had very few families. One of the things I decided to do was to "feature" a different family each week. I would ask them to sit in the front pew, bring up the gifts and have a prayer said for their families and friends. Many times, I would do it spontaneously, without notes.

One Sunday, it was the Adams family's turn. They were seated in the front pew. I finished the homily and the Creed and began the Petitions. I prayed for the Pope, Bishop McDonough and the leaders of the Church. I prayed for world peace. I prayed for all the churches of the county. When I got to the part where I was to pray for the family of the week, I said, "Let us pray for all the families of the parish *except* the Adams family." I thought they were looking at me oddly the rest of the Mass. I was clueless of the mistake I had made.

GET OUT!

One of the first things I wanted to do when I arrived in Monticello, Kentucky, to pastor Saint Peter Mission Church was to join the local Ministerial Association. I was soon invited by the local Southern Baptist minister.

The meeting was to be held at the Independent Baptist Church directly across the street from the Southern Baptist Church. I wore my new Roman collar and black suit because all of the other ministers were dressed in their suits and ties. When I entered the room where the meeting was to be held, the host minister of the Independent Baptist Church suddenly left the room. Several minutes later, his secretary came back into the room with a handwritten message from that minister. It read, "I can no longer in conscience be a part of this group now that it has a Catholic in it. Please leave my church!" The group froze for a minute, not believing what they just read. I prepared myself to make a graceful exit. The Southern Baptist minister intervened and invited the rest of the group to walk across the street to his church to hold our meeting. We never discussed his action, but simply proceeded with the meeting as if nothing had happened.

WAITING FOR ELECTION RESULTS

Most of southern Kentucky was "dry" when I served down there, meaning that it was illegal to sell liquor. The ministerial association, comprised of mostly Fundamentalist church ministers and of which I was a member, became almost apoplectic every time it made it on the ballot during local elections. There were a handful of us young ministers who thought the whole thing was hypocritical because booze was flowing everywhere – some bootlegged and some was bought at the closest liquor store, often several miles away in a wet county. Each time the vote came up, it kept getting closer and closer to passing, which drove the ministerial association up the wall. I think liquor sales finally became legal a few years ago, long after I was gone from the area.

I remember being invited to my Presbyterian minister friend's house, along with two or three other young ministers, to await the results of one of those elections. He served cold beer as we listened to the radio. One minister, who was being interviewed, noted that "there were even a few ministers who backed legal liquor sales" as if our stance was the epitome of sin. At that point in his interview, we cheered loudly, clinked our beer bottles together in a toast! Legal liquor sales did not make it that year, but I think that was the tastiest beer I ever had in a minister's house.

GOTTA ADMIRE THOSE CATHOLICS!

When we were about to open Good Shepherd Chapel in McCreary County in the 1970s, we started by trying to identify if there were any Catholics living in the County. Typically, we found a handful of people who had migrated from cities in the north. However, there was a couple who were obviously born and raised in the area – Arnold and Sally Calhoun. They were mountain people with big hearts. Arnold could do some carpenter work, so he helped remodel the old garage into a chapel. Sally helped the mission Sisters with sorting clothes for the poor and other social service projects.

One day, my curiosity got the best of me. I asked Arnold about his Catholic background. He told me that he had spent some time in "the pen" (penitentiary) for "moonshinin'." While in "the pen," he told me that he had met the Catholic priest chaplain. I pushed some more. "Arnold, you met several chaplains from many different faiths, why did you choose to become a Catholic?" "Well, Father, when people around here want to take a drink, they go out behind the woodshed or into the corn crib and hide it. What I like about Catholics is that don't mind sinnin' right out where you can see them!"

THE (MINISTER) DOTH PROTEST TOO MUCH, METHINKS!

Psychologists will tell you that the more extreme, rigid and self-righteous a person is about an issue of morality, the more likely it is that they have something to hide.

This was no doubt true of a fiery minister I knew about in Pulaski County when I was a young priest. He would rant and rave almost every day on the his radio program about "sexual promiscuity in our culture." He was obsessed about it enough to schedule a bonfire in front of his church and invite everyone to bring their pornographic books and movies to be burned. He even included "women's pantsuits" for good measure.

His bonfire went off OK the following Sunday, but on Monday he ran off with the church's teenage organist!

IS IT FREE?

At the new mission chapel in Whitley City, Kentucky, we were fortunate to have two Sisters of Saint Joseph who were home health nurses to work in the mountain communities of the county. They were successful in attracting a few doctors who were willing to offer their services each month in a free clinic.

Many of their patients were simple, uneducated mountain folks. One of the Sisters told me about a situation she encountered with a woman who had come in to be treated at the clinic. In the preliminary background paper work, one of the questions the Sister asked was, "Have you ever had intercourse?" There was a long pause. The woman responded, "I don't reckon I have, but if you give it to me I am pretty sure my free medical card will pay for it."

POPE JOHN THE BAPTIST?

When we opened the new mission chapel in Whitely City, Kentucky, we knew there were less than ten Catholics in the whole county. Most people had never met a Catholic and knew little about Catholics. Right after Pope John Paul I died, one of the Sisters who was a home health nurse asked a local woman what she thought about the passing of the first Pope John Paul in such a short few days after he was elected. Her response was, "Well, I am sure he was a good man, but I hope they choose a Baptist this time!"

HAVEN'T BEEN TO CHURCH FOR A WHILE, HAVE YOU?

A man and his wife, the Benelli's, had moved to Whitley City from the northeast years before for some reason unknown to us. He had been a confectioner (candy maker) before he retired. They had not been in a Catholic Church for years. They were certainly not familiar with the post-Vatican II liturgy.

Mr. Benelli was very hard of hearing and his eye sight was not too good either. When we got to the Sign of Peace and people were shaking hands, he put on his coat, thinking it was the end of Mass. Then he said very loudly, "I had a great time. Thank you all very much for inviting me." We had to invite him to sit back down.

When it came time for Communion, he got in line, but when he got right in front of me standing there with a plate of communion wafers, he thought it was time for the collection. He dropped a handful of loose coins on the communion plate.

After communion, when everything got very quiet, he started looking around. He noticed the young African American men from the Job Corps Center, where one of the Sister's taught math. They were very burly guys from the inner cities of New York and Boston. We were the only church in the County that welcomed them. He said at the top of his voice, "I didn't know we had "darkies" in our parish!"

The whole room froze and there was a deadly silence. Our guests seemed to take the racist comment in stride, realizing that he was an old man who didn't know any better or they were used to such racial remarks.

WE'RE GOING TO HAVE TO LET YOU GO

One Saturday night, when I was pastor of Holy Name of Mary Parish in Calvary, Kentucky, I had one of my strange dreams about being caught unprepared. They are usually about getting to the pulpit and realizing that I did not have my homily.

This time I was in the sacristy trying to get vested for Sunday Mass. For some reason, I could not figure out how to get into them. My head would come out the sleeve or my arm out of the neck or I would have the alb inside out. I feverishly tried one thing after another, but to no avail. Finally, the bell rang for Mass time and I was still not dressed. Twenty more minutes went by and I was still struggling. I could hear the congregation coughing and nervously twitching as they waited and waited.

Finally, the Parish Council president went to the microphone and called me out of the sacristy to stand in the middle aisle. I shuffled out of the sacristy with my alb wadded up around my shoes. Standing in front of the altar, I heard him say, "Father Knott, we are going to have to let you go. You just can't do it anymore. You have lost it!

As always, I woke up drenched in my own sweat, relieved this time that I had not been fired after all.

DO YOU WANT FRIES WITH THAT?

In preparation for a Confirmation at Holy Name of Mary Parish, I asked those to be confirmed to know the Pope's name, the Bishop's name and the Pastor's name, among other things, just in case Bishop Maloney would ask them during his homily the night of their Confirmation. I thought it would be a good idea at CCD class to have a rehearsal. "The Pope's name is John Paul. The Archbishop's name is Thomas McDonough. The Pastor's name is Ronald Knott." During the second week of preparation, I asked "Who is the bishop?" One little girl was waving her hand wildly, so I called on her. Even though she had everything scrambled, she answered proudly, "Ronald McDonald!" Thomas? Ronald? McDonald? McDonough? It was just too much for her.

UNFORGIVABLE MEMORY LOSS

One of the biggest mistakes I have ever made in all my years of ministry occurred in Calvary.

There was a lovely woman parishioner in a mixed marriage who had finally convinced her husband to allow her to baptize their child. I readily agreed to do it, made all the preparation and set the date. Family members were coming from far and wide. I was going to do it at 1:00 on Sunday afternoon.

When the last Mass was over that Sunday, I totally forgot about it and left for the lake about an hour away. Back then, not much was happening in the parish, so I could normally remember everything without writing it down.

The resistant husband, his relieved wife and her family all showed up at the church, bit I was nowhere to be found. It wasn't until that evening that it dawned on me that I had ruined the most important baptism of all my years as a priest. I was completely beside myself with regret. I paced the floor for hours. I decided that I would not call her on the phone to apologize, but go to the bank the next morning where she worked and try to apologize in person. She was visibly hurt and angry. I apologized profusely and asked her to forgive me. She was stiffly polite, but she never called to reschedule the baptism. It still bothers me to this day. I have never gotten over it and she probably hasn't either – and I don't blame her.

BE CAREFUL WHAT YOU PRAY FOR

In Calvary, the farmers frequently asked me to pray for rain. One Sunday after hearing such a request, another farmer butted in and said, "Now wait a minute. A few years ago we needed rain and we went into the church and lit one of those thirty day candles. It started raining like mad. After about a week of rain, we had to go in there and blow it out!"

JUST DOING WHAT WE'RE TOLD

I have always believed in altar girls and in every parish I have served, I have introduced them as soon as possible, even when the Vatican was unclear about their approval.

I still remember the day the first girl servers were doing their ministry at Holy Name of Mary Parish in Calvary, Kentucky. I would whisper prompts all through Mass, especially when they tended to forget what came next.

After they had brought over the wine and water cruets and I had emptied them into the chalice, I whispered, "Wash hands." This was a signal to bring the water cruet, a bowl and towel back to the altar so I could wash my hands as per the dictates of the ritual before going on with the Mass.

After I finished the offertory prayers, I turned around expecting to see them standing there with the water cruet, bowl and towel ready to wash my hands. They were nowhere to be seen. However, I could hear the sound of water running from the sacristy. I leaned back to take a look. There they were at the sink in the sacristy washing *their* hands!

THE THINGS YOU DO WHEN YOU LIVE ALONE

When I was pastor of the little country church in Calvary, Kentucky, I was often the recipient of some wonderful home-made baked goods. As a result, it was hard to stay on a diet there.

One day, a woman known for her enormously tall German Chocolate cakes, brought one of those monsters to the rectory. I decided that I would freeze it so that I would not be tempted to eat it until some special occasion when I had friends to help me.

Well, I did not make it through the second night. About 2:00 am, I woke up hearing that huge German chocolate cake calling my name from the freezer.

I got out of bed and took the cake out of the freezer with the thought of cutting a small slice, rewrapping it and putting it back into the freezer. No knife would cut it. Desperate to have a slice with a glass of cold milk, I got a large butcher knife and a hammer and finally hacked my way through the hard cake until I was able to remove a nice slice. I rewrapped the cake and put it back into the freezer. I think, as frozen and cold as it was, it was the best piece of cake I have ever eaten.

I could hear it calling me from the freezer every night afterwards. Diet or not, I went through the same process every night until it was gone.

THE ENVELOPE, PLEASE!

When I left Holy Name of Mary Church in Calvary, after three short, but intensely enjoyable years, the people gave me the traditional cake and punch reception with lots of good-bye cards.

I decided that I would give them a party myself to say goodbye. I rented the American Legion Hall, hired a caterer for a buffet dinner and hired a band.

After dinner I solicited two of my most faithful supporters to help me pull off an "awards ceremony." I bought some small plastic trophy cups, copied a picture of my face on some peel and stick paper with the words KNOTTHEAD AWARD. I then spent several weeks thinking of people that I wanted to award with the KNOTTHEAD trophy. I came up with about 75 names – some individually and some in groups.

I then placed the category of the award on envelopes and put the winner's names inside. For example, here are just a few of the categories:

"For the person who slept the most during a homily"

"For the nosiest two women in the parish"

"For the most aggravating question ever asked a priest"

"For the most repeated story about deer hunting"

"For the best cake ever given to a priest for Christmas,

"For the biggest pot crop busted this year"

"For the person who comes to church the latest each week"

"For the people who always leave before Mass it's over"

After reading the category, I would ask one of my women helpers on the stage for "the envelope, please." I would ceremoniously rip the envelope and read the name. They would come to the stage to get their KNOTTHEAD trophy and pose for a quick photo.

It was a howling success. The people were practically rolling on the floor with laughter. The KNOTTHEAD trophies became as prized as an Oscar in Hollywood. What was most amazing was that the whole ceremony was taped and after I was gone, several people held KNOTTHEAD AWARD parties. They would invite people in, have food and re-watch the awards ceremony and laugh all over again.

TALES FROM THE CATHEDRAL

When I was new to the Cathedral as its pastor, I was in my late thirties and new to working in the city. I was from the country and had been pastor at two rural parishes. I was a little naïve about the craziness I would encounter in a center city parish.

THIS IS NOT KANSAS, DOROTHY

I still remember my first day as pastor of the Cathedral of the Assumption in Louisville. I was hardly unpacked when someone at the door was telling the secretary that there was a "streaker" in the Cathedral. She described a "street person with a red shirt in his hands."

A couple of us ran over to the Cathedral see what was happening and to assess what we could do about it. When we got there, all we could see was an older man with a back-pack. Thinking that the mysterious "streaker" had fled, we returned to the rectory offices.

Minutes later, an elderly woman arrived at the door, visibly shaken. "There is a man over in the Cathedral with no clothes on! He has a green shirt in his hands!" Again, we hoofed it over to see what was going on. When we arrived, all we could see was the same older man, fully dressed, with a backpack.

"That's him!" the woman shrieked. What we had was a "street person" changing his clothes from his backpack.

It was only the first of many run-ins with the downtown "street people." Having just arrived from pastorates in the missions and in the country, I remember saying to myself, "Dorothy, you are not in Kansas anymore."

WELCOME TO THE CATHEDRAL

On that same first day as the new Cathedral pastor, I went over to the church at the set time to hear confessions. It coincided with the end of the work day for people working downtown. As I entered the church from the sacristy, I was met by a drunken, one-legged man who wanted to go to confession. My response was, "You are in luck. I am headed toward the confession box right now." More than a bit inebriated, he yelled at the top of his voice, "I want to go right here!" Not used to such an angry response, I immediately dropped down and sat on the high altar steps as he lay there next to me with his one leg and abandoned crutches.

We were both laying on the steps as he started his confession. Just about the time he was in the middle of telling me his sins, I could see two old ladies approaching. When they got within hearing range, I heard one of them say to the other pointing to me before disappearing into the church, "I don't know who the drunk is, but I think the young one with the beard and both legs is our new pastor."

As they disappeared, the man leaned back and noticed the huge crucifix hanging over the altar. "Hey! That's Jesus!" Trying to keep things from deteriorating further, I tried to agree. He did not fall for it. He yelled even louder, "That's not Jesus! That's a ****** cheap copy!"

At this point, having had enough, I handed him his crutches and escorted him to the door. Like the Temple in Jerusalem in Jesus' day, in any downtown Cathedral you see just about anything.

SHE REALLY FLUNKED SPELLING

I think it was my first Sunday as pastor of the Cathedral of the Assumption. I had inherited the former pastor's sister as the parish secretary. She was a kind and helpful woman, but her secretarial skills left a lot to be desired.

One of her jobs was to print the parish bulletin on Fridays before she left work. I had asked her to list the priests who would be giving the homily at each Mass on the weekend. I brought the stack of bulletins over to the church on Saturday when I was to start hearing Confessions. As I sat in the confessional waiting for penitents, I decided to review the weekend bulletins she had printed off.

There it was! Instead of "homilist," she had typed "homolist." Across one page under the word "homolist," she had listed our names: Father Griner, Father Vest and Father Knott.

I shredded all of them. Without bothering to give a reason, I announced at all the Masses that we would not be having a bulletin that weekend.

THE END OF THE WORLD

It had been a very busy week at the Cathedral. I decided to go to bed early to get a little rest. Wrong! About an hour after I had dozed off, the rectory telephone rang. (When the phone rings that late at night, everyone agrees that you are the pastor.) The caller was a panic-stricken, rural-sounding man with a house full of kids screaming and yelling at each other in the background. He had gotten my number out of the Yellow Pages. "Reverend, is the world going to come to an end tonight?" he asked. In my groggy state, I presumed it already had.

After ten years in the Bible Belt as a home missionary, I had handled enough of these calls to know that a long discussion on biblical exegesis would not work. This man needed a "yes" or "no" answer from an authority - now! So, without hesitation, I answered with all the authority I could muster at that late hour. "No, sir, the world will not end tonight. Please go to bed."

He put his hand over the receiver to deliver my verdict to his screaming brood: "He said it wasn't going to end tonight!" There was a lot of muffled arguing before he came back on the phone. "The kids came home from school today saying some preacher had predicted the end of the world and all the other kids were talking about it. They won't go to bed until you talk to them." Believe it or not, I had to talk to five kids, one by one, and tell them in my most confident voice: "Go to bed, honey! The world is not going to end tonight." The father came back on the line, thanked me, and hung up. I was so pleased with myself that I thought I would never get back to sleep.

CLEAN UP IN AISLE NINE

When I first arrived at the Cathedral, we had no full-time janitor – just a young man on the weekends who cleaned the church before the Sunday Masses.

We had a problem with street people messing up the restrooms in the back of church, so we started locking the door when Mass was not going on. This aggravated some of the street people, one of which thought we needed to be punished. He defecated on the carpet right inside the front door one Wednesday afternoon. I noticed it when I went over to hear daily confessions at 4:00 pm.

Having no janitor, I recruited Father Bill Medley to go with me to clean it up before someone stepped in it. With dust pan and broom in hand, we approached our task. Before we reached it, Father Medley suggested that we throw some of that stuff you put on vomit to help absorb the liquid. Bad idea! He started throwing the sawdust-like concoction, but the air-conditioners blew it everywhere but where he intended.

As we approached our target, but just as we got there, Father Medley started gagging. This caused us to start laughing uncontrollably – so much so that we ran down the steps and out the front door to the sidewalk. As we stood there laughing, a woman walked by and saw us. “This has to be the friendliest church in Louisville. I know you stand out here to greet people every Mass on Sundays, but this is Wednesday!” We started laughing again, even harder.

We managed to deal with the unpleasant situation, but I don’t think we stopped laughing all evening.

OY VEY!

Several years ago, I went to one of the local funeral homes to represent the Cathedral at the wake of a man I did not know. I think his wife had come regularly to the weekday Mass when she was working downtown. I did not know either one of them, but the staff thought I should go.

When I arrived at the funeral home I went right into the room directly inside the door. I went up to the casket and introduced myself, telling the family that I was the pastor of the Cathedral and I wanted to express my condolences for their loss. They looked puzzled but expressed their appreciation for my coming. After a few minutes of polite conversation about nothing, I shook their hands and left. Their eyes followed me out as they whispered to each other.

As I was walking out the door, I looked to my right and saw the name of the person I thought I had just visited on the door of the *next* room. As it turned out, I had visited the wrong deceased. I thought it was odd they looked puzzled and there were several Jewish symbols on the flower arrangements.

HOLY SATURDAY NIGHT FEVER

The Holy Saturday Easter Vigil is a long and complicated service which can go on for three hours or more. A whole bunch of things can go wrong under those circumstances.

At one of those celebrations, one of the readings stated that "the angel grabbed the flaming brazier (pronounced "brāZHər") from the altar." However, the lector solemnly proclaimed that "the angel grabbed the flaming *brassiere* from the altar." A brazier is a pot that holds lighted coals. A brassiere is a woman's under wear item. It makes a big difference which one an angel grabs from an altar, flaming or not. The laughs were audible!

At another one of those services, Father Joe Vest, the associate pastor, was in charge of the whole event because he was training the RCIA candidates. He got the idea, a good idea in itself, to add the names of the Catechumens and Candidates to the Litany of the Saints. Obviously, Father Vest did not care whether the names were saint's names or not. He added everyone's name anyway. During the singing of the Litany of the Saints, Archbishop Kelley was at his chair. I was on his left and Father Vest was on his right. When the cantor got to "Saint Buffy" and "Saint Bruce," the Archbishop looked at me with eyes that could kill. I looked at Father Vest with eyes that could kill. A pastor cannot always control the uncooked ideas of his associate pastor.

BURN, BABY, BURN

One day, when Archbishop Kelly, Father Joe Vest and myself were living in the Cathedral rectory together, the fire alarm went off. As I looked out on the sidewalk from the second story window, I saw Father Vest standing in front of a big fire truck surrounded by several young firemen, with his wild red hair standing straight up, wrapped in what looked like a Navajo blanket and house slippers with little bunny heads and floppy ears on his feet. Archbishop Kelly came up behind me as I was looking out and asked what was happening. I responded, "Well, the house is on fire, but I would rather stay in here and burn than go out there and join Father Vest! What about you?"

MORE THAN I BARGAINED FOR

As pastor of the Cathedral, I was only one of a few ministers in Louisville who would do a funeral of someone who had died of AIDS. It was so new and scary to so many people.

While the main church was under renovation, I agreed to do such a funeral in the undercroft below the church, even though I did not know the deceased or his partner. In fact, I had not met anyone in the funeral party until they entered the door of the undercroft. I was expecting a casket, six pallbearers and the grieving family. The cantor and I were standing at the bottom of the steps when the doors opened. Down the steps came six young men in tuxedos holding red roses. They looked like Chippendale Dancers. Behind them was the deceased's partner holding an urn of ashes and crying his heart out.

I remember standing there looking at this scene with my jaw on the ground, for what seemed to be a few long minutes. Once I pulled myself together, I whispered to the likewise amazed cantor, “We will get through this. Pull yourself together and let’s give him the best we have to offer.”

WHAT NAME DID YOU SAY?

Little Henry was on his way to the Cathedral for his baptism, when his father began to worry that he had not chosen an actual saint’s name for the child. Knowing that Saint Henry was a good saint, I had researched the name so that I could say something about the baby’s “patron saint” at the baptism.

On his way to the Cathedral, the worried father passed Saint Leonard’s Church. Seeing the sign in the church yard, he realized that he had a solution. “Leonard,” would be his son’s baptismal name!

At the baptism, I asked the parents, as is traditional, ‘What name do you give your child?” I was expecting to hear “Henry,” but his father answered proudly “Leonard,” as if he had cleverly solved the problem of not having named his son after a saint. “Leonard?” I asked. “Leonard?” Looking down at my prepared notes about Saint Henry, I asked, “How would you like to hear something about Saint Henry?” The child’s father, realizing at that moment that Henry was a saint’s name, stammered. “Sure, let’s hear about Saint Henry.” Suddenly, the name “Leonard” went down in flames, never to be mentioned on his son’s baptismal certificate. To this day, however, I still like to ask the father “How’s little Leonard?”

NIGHT OF THE LIVING DEAD

Then there was the “wig sisters,” as I used to call them. They were blood sisters who lived in one of those old, old apartment buildings downtown where a lot of old maids, old bachelors and a collection of unique people who loved downtown Louisville in the olden days resided. Hardly a conversation took place without the mention of Stewarts, the Vatican of department stores in Louisville located at the corner of 4th and Walnut streets (known now as Muhammud Ali Blvd).

One week one sister would wear the gold shoes and the blond wig, while the other sister wore the brown wig and the silver shoes. Then the next week they would switch.

We had several wealthy parishioners who made large gifts every once in a while. We had several who occasionally dropped in a $100 bill in the collection basket. But we also had people like the "wig sisters." Every Saturday about 4:00, as regular as clockwork, the "wig sisters" would show up at the rectory door to deliver their weekly offering in person, They delivered it with the seriousness of a person carrying a huge bag of money that could not be risked to be placed in the collection basket at the Saturday evening Mass. The envelope always contained exactly $1.00 – in quarters. They never, ever skipped a week. Even when the snow was up to the roof, they would call and promise to deliver it "as soon as possible."

They loved going to church. One of them, in particular, would sit there, trance-like, on the edge of her pew, in rapt attention. Once, when one of the Cathedral staff visited them, one sister had tried to feed the other a doughnut. Her sister had been dead for two days – the doughnut was still sticking out of her mouth. In total denial, all the other sister could say was, "She won't eat!"

A HOMILY MIGHT GET YOU KILLED

When I read the story of Jesus giving a homily to an angry crowd in Nazareth it reminds me of the reaction by a member of the congregation to a homily I gave at the Cathedral. The text of the Gospel of Luke says, "On hearing this, all the people in the synagogue were enraged. They drove him out of the town, and led Him to the brow of the hill on which the town was built, in order to throw Him over the cliff."

In those days, we were welcoming marginal Catholics back to church – especially divorced Catholics, non-practicing Catholics and gay and lesbian Catholics. There was a man, a diagnosed schizophrenic, who was part of a group of right-wing traditionalist Catholics who hated what we were doing.

I was in court with him several times when he would violate our restraining order. He would march up and down the sidewalk with a huge sign that read "Welcome to the church of Satan. Pastor approved sexual perversion." I would be out on the sidewalk greeting people who would walk past him with his sign wondering what it was all about.

His obsession with the makeup of our congregation escalated to the point that one day he made a direct threat. "If you give that sermon welcoming those people one more time, you will regret it!" I answered and told him that, not only were we going to give it again at the next Mass, but all the weekend Masses."

With that he took his place near the front, close to the pulpit, in the middle of a group of older women. Suspecting something ominous might happen, I went to the sacristy, called the police and left by a back door so he could not see me meeting them at the front door.

An officer went down the side aisle. I went down the middle aisle. Just as we got to his pew, he pulled a knife out of his coat. The officer lunged at him and pushed him to the floor. I yelled to the old ladies to "get back." The man with the knife kept trying to bring the knife up into the back of the police officer so I started stomping on the arm that was holding the knife until he let go of it. The police handcuffed him and led him away to jail.

The law in those days was relaxed enough that he could be let out of jail in a few days. He belonged in a hospital, but his family had not been able to get him committed, even after he had taken a sledge hammer to a BMW because one of the women bridesmaid in a family wedding was divorced. He had also been arrested by the FBI for threatening one of our Presidents. He went into a women's apparel store and threw red paint all over the cloths because he thought they were "pornographic." He was especially disturbed that a women's clothing store was advertising in our bulletin.

He basically harassed me from the shadows for the rest of my tenure at the Cathedral. Some of his family were members of our parish. They were especially weary of what he might do next. It wasn't until he got sick and died that we all felt safe with him no longer on the loose.

I had a Mass for him when I heard he had died. He was crazy, but he was sick. He had suffered from schizophrenia since he was a very young man – and so did his family.

THE LOVE DOCTOR

I never knew what was next when I answered the Cathedral of the Assumption's office phone, especially in the early days. Many people thought they could contact the Archbishop by calling there when they felt they had serious problems that needed addressing from the man at the top. One person called to report the mowing crew at Calvary Cemetery for chipping the corner of the base of a family tombstone. Another called to report a Communion Minister who was seen picking her nose. Still another wanted to report someone they suspected cheating on a "cover all" game at the local parish Bingo hall.

Sometimes, I was just dumbfounded as how to answer those calls. Other times I just made up answers like the time an inebriated teenage girl called late at night about her boy friend problem. He obviously wasn't loving her back as much as she was loving him. "Is love wrong?" she asked in a semi-stupor. I was tired that night and I knew any conversation with her would lead to nowhere and she would likely not even remember she had called in the first place, so I cut to the chase and gave her a one-word answer – "Yes! Now goodnight."

RASH JUDGEMENT

The Cathedral parish was often besieged by requests for help from the many street people who gravitated there. One even asked a bride for a hand-out just as she started her big walk down the aisle. One day, running late for the noon mass, I was heading down the middle aisle when I caught sight of a ragged woman heading toward me, trying to get my attention. My mind automatically went into high gear preparing to turn her down and have her to come back later. Before I could spit out my judgmental speech, she opened her hand to give me some change, saying, "Father, where is the poor box? I want to help the poor." I was speechless and ashamed of myself.

THE BEST SEAT IN THE HOUSE

One day, I was in the Cathedral sacristy getting ready to vest for the noon Mass when I looked out to the sanctuary and saw a drunken man passed out on the bishop's throne. I stood there amazed at what I was looking at, but even more amazed that the fifty or so daily Mass attendees were just sitting there looking at him without anyone making a move to de-throne him. To this day, I regret not holding up Mass for a few more minutes while I ran back to the rectory to get my camera. Today, I would have had a cell phone in my pocket to capture the "moment" for the history books.

MURDER IN THE CATHEDRAL

While I was living with Archbishop Kelly at the Cathedral, we had an unwelcomed night visitor. It started with the Archbishop asking me if the choir was rehearsing late into the evenings one week. I kept telling him that they normally practiced to about 9:00 in the evenings on Wednesday nights only. He kept telling me he thought he could hear organ music coming from the cathedral in the middle of the night. I tried to convince him that it must be music coming from the Galleria, a place of several night clubs in the area behind the Cathedral.

He finally convinced me that he was not just "hearing things," so we conducted a search of the building and discovered that a man had built a "nest" in the bell tower where he could sleep at night. He was able to easily find the organ key on the organ and would play it at will even at midnight or whenever he was in the mood. We cleaned out his nest and had a new lock put on the bell tower door.

It stopped the organ playing, but then he was able to find a way to get into the rectory while we were sleeping! For months we would find evidence that he had been in the house because he would move things around and even leave messages for us!

One night I came home from a very late meeting in Memphis. When I opened the door, my room was filled with fifty or sixty candlesticks from the cathedral and its storage rooms. He had gone through my desk, which was piled with papers and left a message, "Cleanliness is the next thing to godliness."

Another night he was sitting in the rectory TV room on my floor watching TV when Archbishop Kelly came home late from a meeting. The Archbishop asked him, expecting to see me, "who are you?" He answered matter of factly, "Oh, I am a friend of Ron's! I was just going down to make myself a turkey sandwich. Can I get you anything?" "No, I have already eaten. I am going to bed," replied the Archbishop who left him there watching TV. I was not even home that night.

The next morning, Father Griner who was also living there, was coming home early from a trip and actually met this guy coming out of the front door wearing one of my clergy shirts, carrying one of my long camera lenses and his prized home-made cane. Father Griner wished him a good morning, thinking he was someone else's house guest.

One Easter Sunday, the Archbishop told me that he had to go to an overnight meeting that evening and that he would not be home until Tuesday. His words to me were, "He was in the house again last night. Some things were moved around in my hallway. Since you are going to be here by yourself, be sure you lock the iron gates to the courtyard and recheck all the rectory doors."

I was leery of sleeping there in the three story, half a block long building, in downtown Louisville by myself, but I checked all the locks and doors and decided to go to bed early – I was tired from all the Holy Week Services.

I was just about to doze off into sleep when I heard someone come in the front door and race up the steps to the third floor where the Archbishop lived. The Archbishop always parked in the back garage and took the back stairs to his rooms.

Convinced I was in the house alone with this mysterious, maybe dangerous, unwanted house guest, I grabbed some clothes and raced out the front of the rectory in my pajamas with blue jeans, shoes and a tee shirt in my hands. I ran around to the garage, got into my clothes and drove to a friends house thinking I would spend the night.

After about an hour I had misgivings about abandoning the house to a who-knows-what. He could be loading all the computers into his car, spray painting all the walls with spray paint and God-knows what else - and just whose fault would that be? Mine.

My friend and I decided to call a security company to meet me back at Cathedral. When I got there, I was met by an 85 years old security guard! As we were standing on the sidewalk assessing what to do next, we noticed that a light on the third floor where the bishop lived, went off. "He's in there," we blurted out in unity.

The old night guard suggested we call the city police, which we did. In a few minutes a couple of squad cars showed up with the Canine Unit. They brought out the dog and I let them in the front door. We could see lights go on in each floor until they got to the third floor. All of a sudden the German Shepherd dog went wild with his barking. A few minutes later, the police and their dog came back down.

"Well, did you get him? Where is he?" we asked. They looked at me and laughed. "Yes, we got him. He went back to bed."

As it turned out, the Archbishop's meeting had been cancelled. They were digging up the alley to do sewer repairs so the Archbishop could not get to his garage so he parked out front. He came through the front door and ran up the steps to catch part of an opera on TV that he wanted to see. (He was a big opera fan.)

While I was running out of the rectory with clothes in hand, driving to my friend's house, calling the security police and driving back to the rectory, the Archbishop had finished watching his opera and went to bed.

The old security night guard and I realized that we had watched the Archbishop turn off his lights, not a supposed intruder. The Archbishop told me that right after he dozed off, he heard two burly sounding voices outside his room say to each other, "We'll get the SOB if he's in here!" He said he sat up, got out of bed and put on his robe and opened his door. One of the policemen put a revolver on his chest and the dog went for his arm! "Who are you? the police asked. "I am the Archbishop. Who are you? With that the incident was over and we all went home.

The next morning, I was in the kitchen reading the paper when the Archbishop came down. Without removing the paper covering my face, I apologized, explained my thoughts and tried to blame him for not advising me of his change of plans even after warning me to be sure to secure the place. We basically laughed about it – or I did! He had a good story to tell at Confirmations around the diocese about our almost "murder in the Cathedral."

YOU'RE NOT OLD

Archbishop Thomas Kelly OP was known for his sense of humor. He was a master of subtlety. One day, Father Medley, my associate pastor, and I were standing in front of the Cathedral greeting people as they arrived for Mass. It was not uncommon to encounter some strange, often mentally ill, street people.

All of a sudden, a woman across the street, obviously homeless, saw us and started yelling and calling us some of the worst obscenities imaginable. She used about ten of the worst words you could call a person. "You old *#!% blank, blank, blanks!"

When we went back to the rectory, laughing our heads off, we ran into Archbishop Kelly inside the door. He asked, "What are you two laughing about?" I told him we had been called some of the foulest names imaginable by a crazy old woman on the sidewalk. He persisted. "What did she call you?" My answer, I repeated a few times, "I can't tell you. It was too foul." "Oh, tell me," he continued to ask. Finally, I told him that she had called us "old *#!% blank, blank, blanks!" His response was, "You're not old."

MY LAST NERVE

At the Cathedral Rectory, it was not uncommon for street people to ring the doorbell at all hours of the day or night. Before we knew how dangerous that could be, we used to answer the door.

One day, one of the street people rang the doorbell several times within a fifteen minute period – even after we told him that sandwiches would be given out at noon and he would have to wait a few more minutes.

After going to the door and telling him this several times, he laid on the doorbell until I came to the door again. By this time, I was out of patience. I yelled at him through the screen, "If you ring that damned doorbell one more time I am going to come out there and break your hand!" With that, I slammed the door and ran nose to nose into Archbishop Kelly who had come to the door to see what the noise was all about. I was embarrassed to have him hear me. He asked very teasingly, "Is that the way you treat the poor at our door?" I had no defense so I answered, "Yes, Archbishop, a couple of them a week!"

THE TRUCK EXORCISM

One evening, I answered the door (something I would never do as the years rolled by) and there was a strange woman standing there telling me that she had a dream about me being in a terrible car accident. She asked if she could go to the garage and say a prayer over my pick-up truck. Well, being naïve, we went back to the garage and she began chanting something in a native American sounding language. Then she pulled out a sage bundle, lit it and began going around my truck with the smoke rolling out of the bundle like a huge cigar.

As I stood there deeply regretting my decision, the other garage door opened and it was the Archbishop coming home from a meeting. He saw me. He saw the woman. He saw the smoking sage bundle. He saw us surrounding my pick-up truck. He was totally confused. Not knowing how to explain it, I simply threw up my hands and yelled, "Don't ask. Don't even ask!" He shook his head and went to his room. I can't remember if we ever mentioned it again, which I was glad not to do.

FIND YOUR OWN PULPIT, LADY!

I remember one Sunday Lenten Mass in particular at the Cathedral. I know it was Lent because I remember wearing purple vestments when I was presiding and Father Medley was preaching.

During Fr. Medley's homily, he asked the rhetorical question, "How many of us ever have everything we want?" He was certainly not expecting an answer, but he got one! Out of the congregation came a woman yelling "I do! I do!" She ran out of her pew and up to the high altar and started reading from her hand-held Bible – a passage from the Book of Revelation. At first, I thought it was going to be a staged "dialogue homily," until Father Medley looked as shocked as I was.

No one, neither Father Medley, the cantor, nor the ushers, made a move to deal with the situation that was becoming an obvious case of yet another "crazy taking over the asylum." It was the first time that everyone in the place agreed that I was the pastor and therefore "in charge."

I got up from my chair, went over to her, grasped her gently by the arm and started leading her down the middle aisle toward the back door. The whole church seemed frozen as she and I veered from side to side – her reading loudly from her Bible and me pulling her in my purple vestments.

When we got close to the back door, she yelled out, "Get behind me, Satan! Jesus is coming soon!" Forgetting that my lapel microphone was still on, I yelled back, "He's coming sooner than you think if you don't get out of here!"

The stunned congregation laughed and clapped loudly as I made my way back up the aisle to my chair, straightening my vestments as best as I could as I walked past them and acknowledged their support. Father Medley finished his homily. Mass continued as usual. It was just a "normal day" in the Cathedral. We had many such days back then.

LATE, BUT GREAT FUNERAL

I enjoy presiding at funerals. I'll take five funerals over a wedding any day! As a result, we always gave funerals at the Cathedral special attention. We enjoyed making them "something special" for the families.

In this case, we had prepared special music, a personal homily and recruited hospitality ministers to make sure non-Catholic relatives felt welcomed. The deceased was an African American member of the parish with very few Catholic relatives and friends.

When time came for the funeral, no funeral entourage had arrived at the Cathedral – no casket, no family and no mourners. We just thought they were running late as we were getting more and more anxious.

Finally, we called the funeral home, only to find out that the funeral was not going to be held at the Cathedral, but at the funeral home on Broadway, a ten-minute drive away and they were all waiting on us.

The cantor, keyboard player, server and I grabbed the lectionary, homily and some hymnals and jumped into the handiest car we could find and drove through red lights to get to the funeral home.

When we got there, out of breath and drenched in sweat, we started singing, reading and preaching as unruffled as we could pretend. During my homily I could hear a few "Amens" coming from the congregation. It was like fuel on flames. My voice got louder and more energized as more “Amens” could be heard. Before long I was “really preaching.” The cantor was “on fire” with her rendition of “Amazing Grace.” People were singing and clapping and expressing their approval. It was a far cry from the typical, somber funeral service in a “white” church.

By the time we were finished, I don’t think anyone really knew that we had been waiting in the wrong church. African Americans have more tolerance about starting services a little late. I don’t think anyone realized that we were late, with the exception of the funeral director, who seemed to be used to “going with the flow.”

CAT IN A TREE

Baccalaureate Masses were often held at the Cathedral for a couple of our local Catholic High Schools. One of the priest chaplains, Father Teddy Sans, who presided at the Mass, was famous for his unconvincing toupee. It looked a bit like a dead cat laying on top of his head.

On one particular occasion, we had decorated the empty space behind the altar with leafless trees. As Teddy passed by one of the trees, a branch hooked his toupee and pulled it off his head. He felt nothing. There it was just hanging in the tree. Oblivious to this mishap, Teddy continued with the Mass. The students were laughing so loudly that he finally realized that something was wrong. One of the servers went over, retrieved the toupee from the branch and handed it back to the embarrassed priest who put it back on his head and adjusted it as best he could.

It was a graduation to remember for the students. For me, it was a source of scorn. For some reason, I, not the tree, was blamed for his mishap!

THE FAMILY THAT PRAYS TOGETHER

As pastor of the Cathedral, I was on call for the neonatal unit at Norton Children's Hospital down the street. I would often be called on to baptize little "preemies" in incubators who were hanging on for dear life. This involved a surgical gown, rubber gloves, and eyedropper of sterile water and a small sterile towel. First you removed their little stocking caps about the size of a half-dollar.

One night, I was called because an older baby was brought in also in danger of death. I was to meet the parents in the waiting room where families gathered to wait for news from the doctors. When I walked in, the parents were asleep on the floor on a thin blanket. They were lying face to face, almost nose to nose, on their sides. They were holding one rosary between them. They had fallen asleep saying the rosary together. I was moved to tears by what I was looking at! I just stood there and took it in for a while before I woke them up to go pray with their sick child. I think, even today, that God has a special place for parents of very sick children.

BRUTAL HONESTY

When I accepted Archbishop Kelly's invitation to be pastor of the cathedral I was told I could request an associate pastor. I chose Father Joe Vest because he had a reputation for liturgy, being a monk for a while, and because I wanted to make good liturgy the mission of the Cathedral. He did the early leg work of making that happen.

I learned many things from him. When I got to the Cathedral, I was not all that confident. I may have been scared or clueless. He forced me to make a decision about whether I wanted to lead or not. I would come into staff meetings with an empty yellow pad. He would come with hand-outs. I had the name "pastor," but he knew how to take charge. I knew I had to either kill him or step up to the plate. He forced me into becoming a pastor, in name and in fact.

He taught me about uncompromising honesty, in things big and small. We got a lot done in those years, but our years together were rocky sometimes. We were both high energy, passionate people. The night before he left the Cathedral, I sat down with him and told him that, even though we had had some rough times, I would do it over again. His response was simply, "Well, I certainly wouldn't!" It was so brutally honest that we both laughed.

During a heated community battle over open housing for gay people, I remember watching the news one night with him standing on the courthouse steps declaring to a bank of TV camera's his gay sexual orientation. My jaw dropped to the floor and I knew the cameras would show up at the noon Mass the next day for my comments. That may not have been a great public relations day for the chancery, but his response came from a passion for honesty and a ministry rooted in compassion. Like all prophets who engage in rubbing the community's nose in the truth, he was brutally honest in the face of dishonesty and hypocrisy.

From the moment I picked your book up until I laid it down, I was convulsed with laughter. Someday I intend reading it.

Groucho Marx

Made in USA - Kendallville, IN
1237340_9780996244572
02.22.2021 0945